THE ANTI-RENT WAR
ON BLENHEIM HILL

MAYHAM: THE ANTI-RENT WAR ON BLENHEIM HILL

The roots of today's problems lie in the solutions to problems of yesteryear. For instance, Holland in the early seventeenth century wanted to establish primacy on the North American continent and to exclude England from this same territory. To do this, the Dutch West India Company was authorized to grant large estates to people who would establish settlements of fifty persons within four years. The owners of these granted lands were called "patroons."

This patroon system continued after the English took control in 1664 and after the American Revolution in the late eighteenth century. This seventeenth-century solution resulted in tensions between landlord and tenant in the nineteenth century.

This volume not only details one portion of the anti-rent wars of 1839–1846, but it also shows how social inequality in 1840 upstate New York is related to a Dutch solution to a problem of 1629.

Mayham: *The Anti-Rent War on Blenheim Hill*
Ned Buntline: *Buffalo Bill and His Adventures in the West*
Ned Buntline: *The Rattlesnake, or The Rebel Privateer*
Swantak-Post: *The Valley We Love: Township*

On the cover:

None of the anti-rent flags that symbolized tenant discontent have ever been found, but Mayham's history contains a description of its design: the cover art is a re-creation of that flag.

Robert Hubbell posed in an original calico Indian outfit handed down in his family.

The Anti-Rent War on Blenheim Hill

An Episode of the 1840s

A HISTORY OF THE STRUGGLE BETWEEN
LANDLORD AND TENANT GROWING OUT OF THE
PATROON SYSTEM IN THE EASTERN PART OF NEW YORK

by

Albert Champlin Mayham

Professor of History in the Cortland Summer School,
Author of a Topical Outline in United States History

Illustrated

STONECREST INDUSTRIES

1906 Edition originally subtitled *An Episode of the 40's*
Copyright, 1906 by Albert Champlin Mayham
Published by Frederick L. Frazee
Jefferson, N.Y.

Centennial Edition
© 2006 by Stonecrest Industries
Published by Stonecrest Industries,
152 Starheim Road, Stamford, NY 12167

www.stoncrestindustries.com
Printed in the United States of America

3 5 4 2

ISBN 0-9712057-6-0

Albert C Mayham

Dedicated to all Blenheim Hill folk in general
and one Thomas Peaslee in particular

Contents

To the Reader
of the Twenty-First Century

Mayham's 1906 edition of *The Anti-Rent War on Blenheim Hill* uses names, locations, and maps unknown or confusing to the reader of 2006.

This section is meant to clarify the original text for today's readers and to seek further details from them—to bring Mayham's history into the twenty-first century.

Please send us questions you may have on this local history, and forward local knowledge. Both will be included in future printings, turning Mayham's *The Anti-Rent War on Blenheim Hill* into a perpetual work-in-progress—a living history with new questions and fresh insights.

You can contact us at Mayham, c/o Stonecrest Industries, 152 Starheim Road, Stamford, NY 12167; or email mayham@stonecrestindustries.com. As we prepare future printings, we will update these notes and send you a copy of these changes.

Maps of the area

The action that Mayham describes takes place over a larger area than that between North Road and Shew Hollow Road. We have therefore included a map of Blenheim and Gilboa so the modern reader can visualize more of the action in this area.

Blenheim and Gilboa *(from the Schoharie County map)*

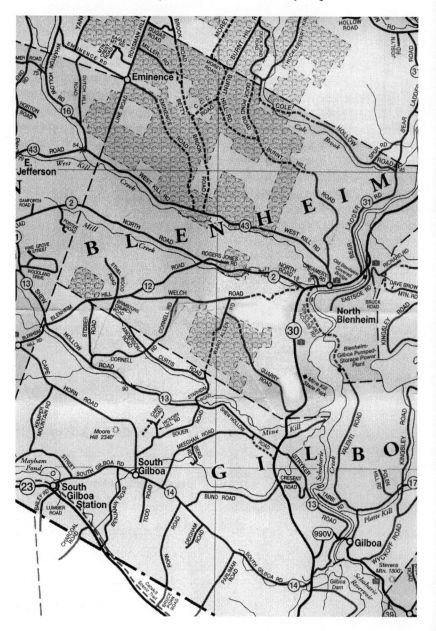

In addition, the original book has a map of the South Gilboa area which has gotten out of date. Two versions of this map show how the roads of 1840 relate to those of 2006.

Country roads in South Gilboa (ca. 1845)

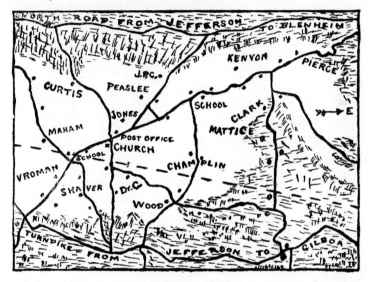

Country roads in South Gilboa (ca. 2006)

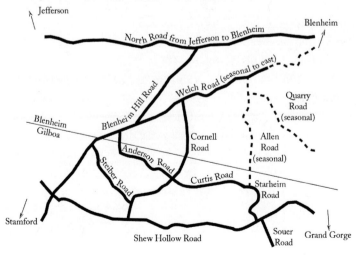

Country roads, 1845 compared with 2006

The top map shows the roads of 1845 and appeared in the 1906 edition of *Anti-Rent War on Blenheim Hill;* the map below it is a tracing showing the road names of 2006.

There are some discrepancies: there had been a road trending south from the Brimstone Church to the Jefferson-Gilboa Turnpike (Cornell Road was roughly parallel to it to the east). This road has become a logging trail, with Cornell Road bending to the west, joining Steiber Road, and then going south in the path of the earlier road to Shew Hollow.

Aside from this, the pattern of roads remains today, though some are now seasonal and many have changed names.

Miscellaneous facts and queries

Backbone: "In the earliest deeds and contracts, Blenheim Hill is call the 'Backbone.'" (Mayham Series)

Baldwin's Mill, Baldwin's Heights: About 4 miles west of Blenheim via West Kill Road.

Black Hawk: Christopher Decker of Blenheim Hill.

Blenheim Church: See Brimstone M.E. Church.

Blenheim Hill Church: See Brimstone M.E. Church.

Brimstone Meeting House: See Brimstone M.E. Church.

Brimstone M.E. Church: The congregation of this church first met at a building on Blenheim Hill Road at the junction with Anderson Road. This *Brimstone Meeting House,* ". . . was built as early as 1815 but not finished inside. . . . In 1835, the church received its name of 'Brimstone Meeting House' [when] the building committee expended all the money subscribed and was unable to paint it white, so decided to use a less costly paint, a cream color. . . . On the question of color, William Baker testified that it was a brimstone color." (Mayham Series)

"In the summer of 1854 the church was rebuilt by A. C. Morehouse and enlarged to 32 × 46. The cost was $1000. It was . . . named the Heding M.E. church . . ." and later again rebuilt and named the Blenheim Hill church. Finally, the congregation's size allowed a church to be built at Blenheim village and another at Shew Hollow; the three churches became known as the Blenheim Church, the Brimstone M.E. Church, and the Shew Hollow Church.

Burnt Hill: An area north of the West Kill Road in Blenheim.

Dutch Hill, Dutch Hill Road: In the northeast corner of Jefferson, to the southwest of Eminence.

Fink's Tavern: At the time of the first printing, we had been puzzled about the location of Fink's Tavern. Lillian Wilson and Beatrice Mattice have since told us that the original foundation is on the west side of Route 30, just north of West Kill Road and before the turnoff for Riverview Cemetery and Wilson's Golden Oak Farms. Part of the building was moved up the hill behind the foundation and remodeled into the Wilson home (the original ballroom stairs now access the Wilson's basement) and the carriage house is now incorporated into the farm buildings.

　　This is confirmed by *Blenheim History 1710-1991* by Fanchon Dewell Cornell and Alicia Tara Cornell, 1994, p. 274.

Gilboa: At the time of the anti-rent wars, Gilboa was the largest town in the county.

Head of the river: The village of Stamford. (Swantak)

Mayham Series — Blenheim Hill: Mayham collected a set of records that was published originally in the *Jefferson Courier and Schoharie County Chronicle* between 1904 and 1907. These are now available in PDF format at http://www.rootsweb.com/~nyschoha/blenheimhill.html. They are invaluable for tracking the history of this area.

Red Jacket: Henry A. Cleveland of Dutch Hill in Blenheim.

Ridge, Ridge Road: Now South Gilboa Road.

Roscoe's A History of Schoharie County, 1713-1882: This book was originally published in the late nineteenth century by D. Mason and Company in Syracuse, and is now available in html at http://www.rootsweb.com/~nyschoha/roscoes.html. Chapters 4 and 16 are especially relevant.

Shew Hollow Church: See Brimstone M.E. Church.

Stage coach stop: The remains of the barn where horses were switched at this stage stop are evident on the south side of Shew Hollow Road between Cornell Road and Starheim Road in a beautifully laid-up stone foundation.

Swantak's The Valley We Love: Township: A history of the valley called Township, to the south of Stamford and east of Hobart. A republication is available from Stonecrest Industries.

Tecumseh: John McEntyre of Gilboa.

West Sand Lake: A village to the southeast of Albany.

Wigwam councils: The group decision-making by the Indians.

Yellow Jacket: Jesse M. Cornell of South Gilboa.

Please write us with questions, information, or if you simply want to be on the mailing list for these updates.

*T*his Indenture made the twenty-eighth DAY of June in the year of our Lord one thousand eight hundred and two BETWEEN Lucus Elmendorf of Kingston, in the County of Ulster and the State of New York, of the first part, and Daniel Wallace, the Second of Blenheim, in the County of Schoharie of the second part, WITNESSETH * * * * ALL that certain FARM piece or parcel of land containing ninety-five acres and an half TO HAVE AND TO HOLD forever, saving and reserving all Mill seats with two Acres of Land adjoining the same and exclusive rights of erecting mills and mill dams thereon, and also all mines, minerals, and ores * * * * * the yearly rent forever of fifteen bushels and an half of good sweet Merchantable Winter Wheat on the first day of January yearly to be delivered in the town of Kingston aforesaid or at some other place equally near the said premises above granted as shall be annually appointed by the party of the first part his heirs or assigns in and upon the first day of July of each year * * * * * If it shall so happen, that the rent above reserved, or any part thereof, shall be behind or unpaid by and for the space of sixty days, then in every such case it shall and may be lawful to and for the said party of the first part, his heirs and assigns or any of them, at the option of the said party of the first part, either to prosecute for the recovery of the same in some court of record, or in person, or by his or their servant or servants, bailiff or bailiffs, into the whole or any part of the premises to enter, and there to distrain, and the distress so taken to lead, drive, or carry away, and the same to expose to sale at public vendue, and out of the monies therefrom arising, to deduct the rent then due and in arrear, together with the costs of distress and sale. * * * * * *

AND PROVIDED FURTHER if it shall at any time happen that no sufficient distress can be found upon the premises to satisfy such rent due and in arrears, it shall and may be lawful to and for the said party of the first part, into the said hereby granted premises to re-enter, and the same as in the estate to have again, re-possess and enjoy; and the said party of the second part, his heirs, executors, administrators and assigns, and all others, thereout and from thence UTTERLY TO EXPEL, PUT OUT AND AMOVE.

Lucus Elmendorf
Daniel Wallace the Second

Sealed and delivered⎫
in the presence of ⎭
  James Brown
  Daniel Broodhead Junr

Preface

Land tenures have been at the bottom of a large part of the social and economic troubles in all ages. The Licinian laws of Rome (367 B.C.) provided that no person should hold more than five hundred jugera. (A jugerum was about half an acre.) By the time of Tiberius Gracchus this law had long since become a dead letter. The Agrarian law advocated by him (133 B.C.) proposed to take away from the great proprietors (the greater part of Italy was then owned by two thousand persons) all the lands they were occupying over and above the amount named in the old Licinian law. The lands thus resumed by the state were to be allotted in small holdings to poor citizens and made inalienable. The aim was simply to put the people into possession of their own. Holders of these lands, long in undisputed enjoyment, had come to look upon them as absolutely their own. Money-lenders who had made loans upon them opposed all efforts to disturb the spurious titles.

This new land law effected a great amelioration of the distress among the poor, and large districts that had been almost depopulated, again became covered with cottages of sturdy peasants. Italy seemed in a fair way of being redeemed from the curse which the monopolization of the soil by the rich had brought upon it. But history repeats itself. In the fifth century after Christ, as in the time of Tiberius Gracchus, the great masses who tilled the soil had not a clod that they could call their own.

The same conditions prevailed in France before the Revolution. The nobility with its 80,000 families, pensioners of the king, ornaments of the court, living in riotous luxury, held one-fifth of the lands of France and paid scarcely any taxes, while the bulk of the population, some 25,000,000 persons, lived by hard labor and lived in want. Whenever the peasant's property changed hands, the lord stepped in to claim his fine. On the roads and at the bridges the lord claimed his tolls. At the markets and fairs the lord claimed his dues and sold to the peasant the right to sell to others the produce of his farm. The peasant must grind his wheat at the lord's mill and crush the grapes in the lord's winepress. The lord alone could fish in the stream which flowed through the peasant's farm, or shoot the game which ruined the peasant's crops. The lord alone could hunt over the peasant's land and deer and big game, preserved for the sport of princes, wandered unchecked, devouring the fields and vineyards of the poor people, and woe be to the peasant who dared to interfere with their freedom. For six months in the year the farmers were compelled to watch all night in order to save their vines and harvests from destruction. When the lord was done with the peasant, the Church stepped in to take its tithe for spiritual purposes, a reminder of how much he owed for the guardianship of his soul. Such conditions brought on the great conflict which destroyed in part the ancient society of Europe and replaced it by a more simple system, based as far as possible on equality of rights.

In all nations and in all ages, any people that prosper must own the soil and live close to it. History repeats itself because man does not change. The same laws obtain today that have been in operation throughout eternity. The same causes work out the same results. Our fathers and grandfathers, sixty years ago, read the history of Rome and of France and stood for their own right to the soil on Blenheim Hill. The purpose of this history is to set forth the struggles of a noble generation for the legal possession of what was theirs by natural right. I am not conscious of approaching the subject with a bias in favor of either landlords or tenants, though both my grandfathers belonged to the anti-rent party and I was to the manor born. I have tried to summarize the economic and political aspects of the agitation that I might have more space for the story of what the people thought and felt and did.

In the preparation of this book I am greatly indebted to Prof. Thomas Peaslee and Almerin Martin, Stamford; Dr. R. Hubbell and Dr. A. W. Clark, Jefferson; M. V. B. Hager and Freegift Patchin, Blenheim; Hon. S. L. Mayham and Prof. S. Sias, Schoharie; Hon. John R. Sage, Des Moines, and W. H. Gallup, Boone, Iowa; Rev. Joel Warner, Kenesaw, Neb.; Isaac Peaslee, Georgetown, Cal., and many others. My thanks are especially due to the publisher, Mr. Frederick L. Frazee. Not only has he taken great pains in printing the story from week to week in his newspaper, The Jefferson Courier and Schoharie County Chronicle, but he is to be congratulated on the excellent appearance of the book itself, the first turned out by his printery.

I am conscious that the style of the book indicates its method of preparation. Chapters have been written at odd times,—at the noon hour and at midnight, in the study, on trains, and among the hills. Copy has been sent to the printer without revision and in no case have I seen a single proof-sheet.

A. C. M.

Warwick, N. Y.
October, 1906

THE ANTI-RENT WAR
ON BLENHEIM HILL

CHAPTER I

News from Rensselaerwick

The anti-rent agitation which occupied the public mind in the state of New York during the seven years from 1839 to 1846 was a momentous question with the citizens of Blenheim Hill. The hardships of earlier days had passed away. The log houses were snug and comfortable, barns sheltered numerous sheep and cows, and every yeoman owned an ox-team. There was plenty in every household and the spacious fireplaces filled the little homes with warmth and good cheer. A generation of strong men was coming to the fore.

Let us survey the Backbone in the early spring of 1839. Henry Maham was an old man now and paid the most tax in District No. 18. His son John was in the prime of life and the leading man in the community. The Brimstone meeting house was finished and paid for in full. Rev. F. W. Sizer and Rev. Wm. Lull occupied the high box pulpit. Thomas Peaslee was 57, strong in the Methodist faith and settled in his determination to pass the remainder of his days on Blenheim Hill. Benjamin P. Curtis, at 45, had come to be regarded as the head man in the congregation. Thomas Sheldon Peaslee was 33, Milo Wood 36, Col. John R. Sage 29, Giles S. Champlin 26, Daniel Sage 23, and John A. Clark 21 and newly married. Every household had its spinning wheel and nearly every one its little home-made red cradle and among the babies in the latter were Joel Warner, Lucinda Champlin, Isaac Peaslee, and Matilda Sage.

Spring began in March by the almanac but the snow was still three feet deep in the sugar camps and along the highways. Already the farmers were planning for the season's work. Wheat had commenced to fail for in the earlier days when a wheat rent payable in Albany had been the price of a farm, the settlers had cropped the most easily tilled land year by year until the soil no longer produced an average crop. Now, however, payment in kind at Albany has been commuted and a money rent, payable in Blenheim, arranged in lieu of it.

But whence the rent? The farmers of Blenheim Hill had scarcely given the matter a thought prior to that spring of 1839. The new landlord, Mr. John A. King of Jamaica, Long Island, had been frequently among the tenants, treating them with liberality and fairness and the old and troublesome arrears had been adjusted and settled on terms and conditions which all admitted liberal and satisfactory. Surely the people were prosperous and happy. But rent day suggested a fundamental question and the presence of the agent of John A. King caused the thinking men of the community to get back to first principles. Benjamin P. Curtis had played the fife and drum in the war of 1812, a war waged for free trade and sailors' rights. Benjamin P. Curtis and John Mayham met upon the highway one day in the spring of 1839 and stopped to chat together as they let their oxen drink from the spring near which Utsayantha spent a few happy weeks in 1695, the spring which Sheldon Peaslee curbed for the public good.

"Good morning Benjamin," said the keen Irish farmer, "back from Duanesburg are you? What is the best word from the Helderberg country?"

"Good morning John," replied the Yankee, "wait till I gee a little and your oxen can come nearer to the spring. News in plenty there is from Albany. Old Stephen Van Rensselaer died on the 26th of January and left debts to the amount of $400,000. But it is not his creditors who are worried. His tenants are in arrears to fully that amount and the old man has ordered all this back rent to be applied on the payment of his own debts."

"Strange, Benjamin, strange," said the other. "We always accounted Stephen Van Rensselaer a rich man. He did more to improve and settle the vast estates which he inherited than any of his ancestors. I have heard that he was remiss in the collection of rents and in case of favorite tenants, and those who had suffered misfortune or otherwise had difficulty in meeting regular payments, he was in the habit of allowing the rent to run on almost indefinitely."

"But this was a mistaken generousity John, unless the payments were finally to be remitted altogether."

"Right you are Benjamin, for a good share of the $400,000 now due must be rent of many years' standing. It will turn many a man homeless from the land. Did not Van Rensselaer make any provision for the remission of the debt in case of utter inability or of misfortune?"

"Yes, in some cases, so they say, but the tenants as a whole are waiting anxiously to learn just what action will be taken by his heirs and executors. Somehow there is a general disposition to distrust the principal heir, young Stephen Van Rensselaer. They fear he is not the man his father was. They were talking when I left of holding a meeting in the township of Bern to consider what action should be taken and it is likely that they will appoint a committee of their best men to wait upon Mr. Van Rensselaer at the manor house and find out if possible what is to be done about the payment of back rent."

"My father was one of Van Rensselaer's tenants once, and I was born upon his land. When my father lived in County Tyrone, in the north of Ireland, he held a farm under the British tenure of land titles. Now he and you and I and all of our neighbors here hold under the Blenheim patent and must acknowledge a landlord. It seems to me that we should own the land ourselves and pay no rent to anyone. What right has John A. King to the farm that I have carved out of the wilderness with my own hands? What right has he to the improvements which I put upon it year by year? He has never even seen the place, yet I must pay tribute to him year by year and my children after me and this thing must go on, by the terms of the lease, forever."

"Well John, they are talking in just this way over on the Helderbergs and I have been thinking about the matter ever since I got home. I have about made up my mind that this rent business is all wrong. But we are bound to hear more of it from Bern. Something is going to happen over there. The people are talking of nothing else. I saw Mr. Baker yesterday and he is going over there sometime in May. He will have some interesting news when he returns."

Only a few days later or, to be exact, on the 25th of March, 1839, Benjamin P. Curtis, George Elliot, and Joseph Curtis, second, trustees of school district No. 18, all made their way to the home of Isaac Ferguson, about seven in the evening, where they found Stephen Maham waiting for them. The business of the meeting was soon transacted. A deed was properly made out and executed, signed by both Isaac Ferguson and his wife, Abiah, conveying to the trustees of school district No. 18, one quarter of an acre of land on which to build a school house. Stephen Maham signed the deed both as witness and as commissioner and Stephen M. Ferguson also witnessed the indenture. The formal transaction over, all hands fell to visiting and Mr. Curtis again related the news from Albany County. All were deeply interested, not only because the farms of Blenheim were lease land but for the further reason that many Blenheim Hill families had near relatives on the Helderbergs who were likely to suffer through the acts of Van Rensselaer.

Mr. Baker went over in May and there was news enough to be sure. A well attended mass meeting had been held only a few days after Mr. Curtis' visit in the early spring and on the 22d of May a committee of tenants called upon young Stephen Van

Rensselaer. He refused to receive them, to speak to them, or to acknowledge their presence in any way. Though he was sitting in his office when the committee entered, he retired into an inner office where he held a long and confidential conversation with his agent, Mr. D. B. Lansing. The latter at length came out and reported to the committee that Mr. Van Rensselaer would later communicate with them in writing. Here the matter rested.

Haying was well advanced on Blenheim Hill in the summer of 1839 before anything further was heard from the Helderberg country. Then there came a report that Stephen Van Rensselaer had addressed a letter to Mr. Van Dusen, the chairman of the committee that had visited him on the 22d of May, in which he declined selling his lands on any terms, and made no advances toward settling. The effect of this letter was to create a widespread feeling of antagonism and a general determination to resist the collection of all arrearages, should an attempt be made to apply the law. The men of the Backbone discussed these matters fully during the weeks of harvest and again awaited news from Bern, Westerlo, and Rensselaerville.

CHAPTER II

Writs of Ejectment

Late in the summer of 1839, Stephen Van Rensselaer as executor of the estate of Stephen Van Rensselaer, deceased, applied to the Supreme Court for writs of ejectment and of fieri facius against certain tenants in the townships of Bern, Westerlo, and Rensselaerville, in Albany County. These writs were made returnable on the first Monday of January, 1840. Amos Adams, an undersheriff, attempted the service of the first of these writs on the 28th of August, 1839. The news was carried quickly to Blenheim Hill. Haying was in progress and two men were at work in a small meadow now owned by G. S. Champlin and located just south of the field known as the Sage pasture. It was nearing six o'clock. A footman was seen on the road down by the mud bridge.

"By shot John," said the younger of the two men as he glanced toward the highway without slacking his speed, "there comes Henry Cornell on his way back from Albany. He has walked every step of the way today and will be home before sundown, too, if we do not stop him."

"A little rest will do us all good just now Giles," replied the other, "and friend Cornell will have news from over east. It is time to stop work anyway for I have my chores to do yet after I get home," and the two farmers made their way to the road as Mr. Cornell came along. After the usual greeting, the traveler did not wait to be asked for news but volunteered:

I tell you boys there is going to be trouble over in Albany County and it is already well under way. Sheriff Archer sent a deputy out from Albany day before yesterday to serve a writ on a man named Hungerford in one of those cases that young Steve Van Rensselaer is bringing against his tenants. Hungerford showed fight and told the under-sheriff to get right back to Albany and not try to serve any more papers. The fact is the people all through there have made up their minds that none of those writs shall be served and there is one thing about it, if the sheriff tries to send any one around to serve those papers that man is going to get hurt. The under-sheriff did serve several writs and then stayed over night at the Rensselaerville tavern. The landlord was a little uneasy and locked the barn up tight but yesterday morning the sheriff's horse was found with his mane and tail sheared off, the harness was all taken apart, and the wheels on the wagon changed. The under-sheriff took the hint and started back to Albany right after breakfast. I tell you the men are mad around there. They swear they will tar and feather the next constable that comes in sight.

The three men talked earnestly together for a quarter of an hour, after which Mr. Cornell continued his journey down the Burnt Hill to his home on the Minekill, carrying the news of the anti-renters to the little settlement in the valley.

The two men discussed the rent problem as they wrought together on the day following. It was in the days of general trainings when the assembled militia served to give dignity to the State. Men had respect for law. The idea of resisting an officer, civil or military, was not at that time calculated to find favor on Blenheim Hill. The whole matter, so far as it was at that time understood by the young farmers, was carefully studied. At noon time they met a younger brother of one of them.

"Well boys," said he, "I am a Sergeant now; here, read this John," and he handed over a sheet of paper, 8 × 12 inches, from which the person addressed read aloud as follows:

State of New York.
To Mr. George H. Champlin, Greeting:
You have been elected a Sergeant of a Company under the command of Capt. Giles S. Champlin in the 104th Regiment, 28th Brigade, and Sixteenth Division of Infantry of the Militia of the State of New York:—I do therefore, in pursuance of the statute in such case made and provided, Grant you this Warrant. You are to obey the orders which you shall, from time to time, receive from your superior officers, and to discharge the duty of Sergeant in said company, with fidelity, according to the laws and regulations established for the government and discipline of the Militia of this State.
Given under my hand at Blenheim this 20th day of August, A.D. 1839.
Abel Parsons, Colonel

"There Captain," said the reader, handing the paper back to its owner and addressing the man with whom he had been at work all morning, "that sounds like obeying orders, doesn't it? I tell you what, it might happen that the State would call on your regiment to put down an anti-rent mob, what would you do?"

"I would obey, sir," was the reply, in a tone which would likewise command obedience. Then, dropping the military formality, Capt. Champlin continued:

"Old Hickory was not in sympathy with the tariff but when South Carolina began to talk about nullification he let them know down there that the laws must be obeyed. It is the same here. I shall continue to pay rent until the law is changed. What do you think John, will George make a good sergeant?"

The question served to bring back the attention to the newly appointed officer, who carefully folded his warrant, which he had until then held in his hand, and put it, with some other papers, back into his pocket.

John R. Sage mused a full minute before he answered. A comely woman, with an infant in her arms, stepped to the kitchen door and called the men to dinner. As all three turned to go inside, he said: "George is bound to make a good sergeant. He is in your company. He must obey *you*."

So interested had the people of the Backbone become in what was passing on the Helderbergs that means were found to keep in close touch with friends and relatives there. About a month after the attempt to drive off under-sheriff Adams, word was brought to Blenheim Hill that on September 16 had occurred another clash between an officer and a body of angry citizens. On the morning of that day a young man named Leonard served a writ on Paul H. Vincent, who immediately sent a messenger to inform his neighbors that "one of the patroon's men was out serving papers." Soon after Leonard had left the house, Vincent rode past him on horseback and called out to him that if he valued his life he had better return to Albany with all possible speed. At the same time alarms were sounded in every direction. The tenants were rising.

The story of that 16th day of September has been handed down for more than three score years in many a Blenheim Hill family. The officer did not heed the warning given him but proceeded to the house of Andrus Onderdonk and served a writ on him and attempted to make a similar service on James Leggett who refused to take the paper. Leggett, his son, and another man now followed up the officer, threatening to kill him if he served any more papers. A considerable crowd collected about him, shaking their fists in his face and calling him names of which traitor, scoundrel, and villain were the mildest used. At this Leonard gave up the attempt to make any further service and returned to Bern, on his way back to Albany. Here, however, he was met by a company of men on horseback, about fifty, who prevented him from taking passage in the mail coach to Albany, as he desired. Among the crowd were several of those upon whom he had already served declarations, who forced him to go with them and take back the writs. Then they set a tar barrel on fire, and seizing Leonard, brought him to the blazing barrel and forced him to throw all the papers in his possession into the flames. They next took him to Lawrence's tavern and set another tar barrel on fire. Some of the more bold ones threatened to throw him into the fire and did actually cut off part of his hair, but the others interfered and prevented any further violence. After detaining him from nine in the morning until four in the afternoon, they announced to him that he was discharged.

All this made a thrilling story at the stone bees and other gatherings during the autumn of 1839 as the men of Blenheim met together. On the whole they did not approve of the acts of violence and some even went so far as to favor Stephen Van Rensselaer in his course, though they were few. Benjamin P. Curtis, slow and deliberate in matters of importance, reserved his opinion, as did some others of the older and leading men. The time had not yet come for the Backbone to take a decided stand but the questions at issue were being carefully gone over. Mr. Curtis and John Mayham held frequent conferences and both consulted Thomas Peaslee. There were younger men waiting for a declaration from this trio and as yet no declaration came. While they hesitated the year's harvest was gathered in. The forest trees were nearly bare of leaves when the next news came from Albany. This time an itinerant preacher on his way to hold special services in the Brimstone meeting house brought the word. He put up at the home of Thos. Peaslee of course and gave his version of a riot that had occurred on October 16, a version not at all favorable to the anti-rent cause.

CHAPTER III

The Itinerant Preacher

The church has always been more or less in partnership with the aristocracy. The rich are good patrons. The clergy is conservative. Reforms are not generally announced from the pulpit until they have been a long time working in the pews. In matters spiritual the minister may be a long ways in advance of his flock. In temporal affairs the congregation always draws the minister, a reluctant follower. When the anti-rent agitation began in 1839, the preachers, almost without exception, supported Van Rensselaer and denounced the tenants.

As related in the last chapter, an itinerant revivalist arrived on Blenheim Hill towards the end of October and found a welcome in the home of Thomas Peaslee. Aunt Eunice, a dear old lady, spread a bountiful feast for the man of God, in spite of her fifty-seven years. She had been feeding preachers all her life and not a circuit rider in the country but knew her good cookery. The dominie had fasted all the way from the Helderbergs in anticipation of a seat at the Peaslee board and when he reached it he invoked the blessing of Jehovah with fervent lips. Those men of the cloth in the days of Van Buren were men of large capacity in more ways than one and the way they could eat would astonish a modern housewife. On this particular occasion Aunt Eunice witnessed the depletion of her viands with keen satisfaction, for it not only testified to her domestic skill but she felt also that out of the same mouth which now seemed to communicate with some bottomless receptacle, would proceed, measure for measure, words of Gospel fire, when the minister finally stationed himself in the pulpit of the Brimstone meeting house, after his hunger had been appeased.

Supper over, Uncle Thomas opened the Book, read a familiar chapter, and the whole family knelt in prayer, each member taking part. Ah, what a potent factor was the family altar on the old Backbone! How many children were taught to pray there and went on praying all their lives, keeping the Golden Rule, and administering to the necessities of not only saints but sinners also! After prayers that evening the conversation naturally turned to news from Albany County, for Thomas Peaslee was born there and had lived there until 1806. News from the old home was welcome.

Benjamin P. Curtis dropped in that evening and it was during his visit that the dominie related the story of the riot of October 16th, after having gone over the earlier history of the troubles.

"The sheriff came out that morning from Albany with three assistants, intending to proceed to the town of Bern to serve processes. He had traveled about sixteen miles, when he was met in the public highway, at Reidsville, by seventy-five or a hundred men who stopped him and his deputies. In the meantime a general alarm was sent out and men came pouring in from all directions. It was a sinful and excited crowd, brother Peaslee," said the good man, deliberately peeling his third apple as though he had not already disposed of supper enough for two, "a crowd of law-breakers, a mob. In less than an hour it looked like a general training, there had so many men assembled. Finally the ruffians got a tar barrel and set it on fire in the middle of the road in front of the sheriff and his assistants and then two fellows seized the horse and declared that the officer should go no further on business for Van Rensselaer, at which the crowd set up a general hurrah, shouting 'Down with the rent,' blowing horns, and making all the noise possible. The

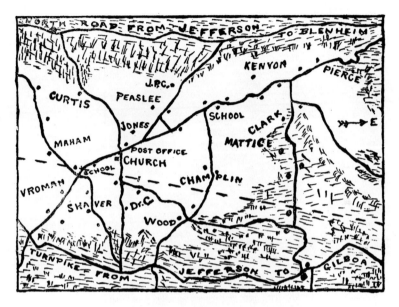

Old map of Blenheim Hill

sheriff commanded the people to give way and let him pass to transact his official business but they utterly defied him and at last he was compelled to give up and return to Albany. It was a great outrage brother Curtis," said the minister as he accepted a plump fried-cake from Aunt Eunice who kept a plate full near the apple pan. "It is the devil's work," he continued as if talking to himself, but neither brother Peaslee nor brother Curtis said amen, for in truth both were contrary minded even then.

In the course of the revival meetings which followed, opportunity was taken to denounce anti-rent sentiment though perhaps with no suspicion as yet that the citizens of the Backbone were already in full sympathy with the movement, or rather with the idea, for the leading men in private conversation did not sanction any acts of violence. With the real issue not yet brought home to them they were able to think of the question of rent in the abstract.

Thomas Sheldon Peaslee

The minister continued to make his home with Mr. and Mrs. Peaslee, although he foraged about the neighborhood with an appetite that made the hardy woodchoppers envious. One night he engaged Uncle Thomas in conversation on the question of Van Rensselaer's claims against his tenants and drew from him an interesting statement.

"We have landlords and tenants right here on Blenheim Hill," said Mr. Peaslee, "and a very good kind too it seems to me. My son, Thomas S., lets a place to John Warner. John has wood for one fire and pasture for two cows and Sheldon furnishes a yoke of oxen and half of the tools. He also furnishes grass to cut to the halves to winter the cows and is to half the expense on wintering the oxen. John has the plow land for three years and barn room for his stock. Sheldon pays him fifty cents a rod for all the stone wall that he builds. It is to be $4\frac{1}{2}$ feet wide

at the bottom and 2½ at the top. He gets 30 cents a rod for split-
ting rails and building fence six rails high with stake and rider.
Sheldon furnishes all the grass seed and half of the other seed.
John has to summer fallow five acres of sward ground for wheat
and five acres for potatoes and do all the work, including thresh-
ing, and have half of the crops. He gathers the apples and has
half, also cultivates a garden on shares. Now there is no written
contract signed between them, and the bargain comes to an end
sometime. John and his children will not have to go on paying
rent forever to Sheldon and his children. The terms of the Van
Rensselaer lease may have been all right in the beginning but
that was more than two hundred years ago. In the meantime,
generations after generations have come and gone, have
worked upon the land and improved it and made it valuable
and the Van Rensselaer family since 1629 has been collecting
rent year by year and may go on collecting rent forever. Sheldon lets John have this land for three years. There is a house
and barn and meadow land and plow land and pasture all ready
for use. What is more, the two men look over the property and
come to an agreement about it themselves. Neither one is
bound by a contract made two centuries ago in Europe when
Kings and companies sold land in America that never belonged
to them at all. I am convinced," and here Thomas Peaslee got up
from his chair and began walking rapidly up and down the floor,
"I am convinced, sir, that this matter of perpetual rent is wrong,
WRONG, WRONG!" and he raised his voice and brought his fist
down upon the table with a mighty thud, as he stopped short in
front of the astonished dominie who had listened attentively,
eating apples and fried-cakes the while.

CHAPTER IV

First Conflict with the Posse

The winter of 1838-39 was very severe on Blenheim Hill. Snow lay six feet deep on the level, traveling was difficult, and oxen were driven tandem. Good crops followed the next summer. On the whole, the farmers of the Backbone had probably never known, up to that time, so prosperous a year. This is a matter of importance. There was no element of discontent to enter into a fair and full consideration of the rent question as it was being presented to them from time to time. When Thomas Peaslee finally declared himself in his spirited speech to the dominie, he had weighed the matter carefully and was in no wise influenced by outside considerations. The question had become a public one now and the Albany newspapers reported it. Those who could afford the Argus got the news week by week and every copy went the rounds of several families. It would be an easy matter to turn to the files of that newspaper and gather the progress of the anti-rent movement. Such files could be found today in more than one kitchen-chamber on Blenheim Hill.

The sheriff, with three assistants, one of whom was Isaac Wynnee, started on Nov. 27 to serve processes in the locality already made familiar in these sketches. When his route became known, alarms were sounded as before, several hundred horsemen gathered, and the attempt was again defeated. Despairing of success in serving his writs with no greater force than the authority of his official position, the sheriff then issued summons for a *posse co-mitatus* to six or seven hundred citizens of the county, command-ing them to report in Albany at 10 A.M. on December 2. Five hun-dred men having reported, they set out immediately for the disturbed districts, some on horseback, others in carriages, others on foot, and all unarmed. Let the story of the day be told in the words of one of the company as he sat before the glowing hearth in Thomas Vroman's spacious kitchen while he tarried over night, the drifts in the Delaware road having stopped him in his journey to the Head-of-the-river.

When we reached Clarksville, some twelve miles from Al-bany, we found about a hundred men gathered on horse-back with others on foot. I was one of a hundred mounted men whom the sheriff ordered to ride with him in advance of the greater part of the posse on our way to Reidsville. I have an idea that the sheriff wanted to see what resistance was likely to be offered and to find out whether the whole posse would be able to get through the crowd for we heard that many farmers had assembled there.

When we got on the Helderbergs, about a mile from Reidsville, we met four or five hundred men on horseback and these were soon joined by the other hundred who had followed us from Clarksville. The crowd closed in upon us and prevented our moving for half an hour but finally let us pass and we pushed on to Reidsville where we found fully eighteen hundred people assembled who entirely filled up the highway and would not allow us to pass. The sheriff went quietly among us and told us to move at a signal from him but when it was given and we tried to force our way the mob made a rush upon us, crying 'stop them,' and it was impossible for us to move. The men were very much ex-cited and nearly all carried clubs. The sheriff saw it would be useless to try to go any further so he commanded us to turn about. We moved slowly out of the crowd but several hundred followed us three or four miles on our way back. It was long after dark before we reached Albany.

Thomas Vroman and his visitor talked until long past midnight on the question of rent and resistance. During the following week he found opportunity to relate the story of his visitor among his neighbors and again there was anxious waiting of news from Albany County. When it came, it told how the sheriff, immediately upon his return to Albany, went directly to Governor Seward at eleven o'clock at night and told him of the day's occurrences, and called upon the executive for military assistance sufficient to enable him to serve the papers in favor of Stephen Van Rensselaer.

After a conference with other state officers, the Governor, on the fifth of December, sent a written reply to the sheriff's application, instructing him to obtain attachments from the Supreme Court for contempt and warrants of arrest from a justice of the peace, against several persons who had resisted him. This he did on December 7. The Governor thereupon directed him to summon as a posse the uniformed military corps of the city of Albany with their arms and equipments, which he did. On the succeeding Monday, at 4 A.M., this posse comitatus, representing the armed power of the county, met at the arsenal. Also, by order of the Governor, two thousand additional men were held ready to march should they be needed. At six o'clock the sheriff at the head of one hundred and twenty men set out. A storm commenced soon after they left the city and continued for twenty-four hours. The roads began to drift badly and in the course of the day became almost impassable. Many persons who had accompanied the sheriff as spectators made their way back through the snow, reporting that several thousand men were gathering in and around Reidsville. Much solicitude was felt for the posse and a number of citizens organized themselves into two volunteer companies and tendered their services to the Governor, if needed.

Meanwhile the posse, upon reaching Reidsville, found that no resistance was offered them but that they could get no accommodations for the night and accordingly fell back to Clarksville. A report of the day's work was sent to the Governor and a request made for tents, blankets, and provisions. Governor Seward then issued general orders converting the posse into a regular military force, but the sheriff returned an urgent message asking for a stronger force. Accordingly, on Tuesday, December 10, the Governor dispatched heavy reinforcements to the aid of the sheriff and at the same time issued a proclamation reciting the unlawful resistance to the sheriff, enjoining all citizens to assist the officers of justice in performing their duty, and appealing to those who had taken part in the recent unlawful assemblies to desist from any further tumultuous gatherings. On Wednesday the sheriff and his strong military escort moved again toward Reidsville. They were met as before by a large assemblage of people. The troops formed in solid column and marched into the midst of the crowd. The sheriff then made one arrest and served a number of writs.

It now became necessary to quarter the troops but the sheriff found that the rent-resisters occupied, as before, all the barns, sheds, and public places, in order to prevent the troops from securing shelter or accommodation. They were ejected, however, and headquarters established at Reidsville, small detachments going out with the sheriff. By Friday this officer had so far made arrests, levies, and service of writs that he reported to the Governor that troops were no longer needed and they were ordered back to Albany, returning on Sunday through deep snow and a blinding storm.

Dr. Cornell was the first man on Blenheim Hill to get a copy of a newspaper containing Governor Seward's message to the Legislature, issued January 7, 1840, and carried it with him on his rounds, reading and discussing it with his neighbors. It was evident that, while the Governor had acted with promptness and severity against the lawlessness, he showed great sympathy and appreciation for the abuses which were its ultimate cause. One part of the Governor's message Dr. Cornell quoted with great favor. It said:

> Such tenures, introduced before the Revolution, are regarded as inconsistent with existing institutions, and have become odious to those who hold under them. They are unfavorable to agricultural improvement, and inconsistent with the prosperity of the districts where they exist, and are opposed to sound policy and the genius of our institutions.

CHAPTER V

Development of Land Tenures

Before considering the elements of the early land policy of the State of New York which gave rise to the anti-rent movement of 1839-46, a clear knowledge of the historical development of our actual system of land tenures becomes a matter of prime importance. There are certain cardinal facts in the history of the English speaking people which can be readily understood by those who lay no claim to a liberal education. In the fifth century after the birth of Christ, there dwelt a free, liberty loving, land owning folk in the narrow peninsula that parts the North Sea from the Baltic. They were an outlying fragment of the English stock, the bulk of whom lay further to the south and east between the Weser and the Rhine and stretching away to the Elbe. They were all low German tribes, a branch of the great Teutonic family.

Land with the German race seems at a very early time to have become the accompaniment of full freedom. The freeman was strictly the free-holder, and the exercise of his full rights as a free member of the community to which he belonged became inseparable from the possession of his holding in it. The villages were separated by strips of forest or waste. Each family of freemen held its own allotment of corn-land and fallow. Woodland and pasture were undivided and every free villager had the right of turning into it his cattle or his swine. The meadow-land lay in like manner open and undivided from hay harvest until spring.

It was only when grass began to grow afresh that the common meadow was fenced off into grass-fields, one for each household in the village; and when hay-harvest was over fence and division were at an end again.

The Roman historian Tacitus, said of the early Germans:

A fine, unmixed, and independent race, unlike any other people, with stern blue eyes, ruddy hair, of large and robust frames, but with a strength which only appears when roused to sudden effort. They will be slaves of no man. Fierce and cruel in war, they are content, when the war is over, to lay aside the sword and spear, and to plow their fields and to cultivate their lands in peace and quiet.

In 449 the vanguard of the English reached the island of England. By 827 they had given their name to the land and had brought thither their domestic, their social, and their political institutions. No sooner, however, had the English become united and securely established in their adopted country than piratical Danes swarmed upon their coasts, planting themselves at various points and waging perpetual war upon the English. For two hundred years the two races struggled for the mastery and finally the Danes won, placing Canute the Great upon the English throne in 1017. The two peoples were alike in parent stock, in language, in religion, laws, and customs, and they easily assimilated. The Danish line lasted only a quarter of a century, when the Saxon line of kings was restored.

William, Duke of Normandy, invaded England in 1066 and seized the crown. This conquest changed the whole system of English land tenure. The English estates were confiscated and distributed among the Norman nobles who had formed a part of William's army, while their former Saxon or Danish owners either found refuge in foreign lands, or, as outlaws, waged a desultory warfare upon their Norman conquerors.

The Feudal System, already prevailing in Spain, France and Germany, a necessary creation of the Middle Ages, was thus brought into England. After the conqueror had parceled out the English lands among his followers, they in like manner divided them among their dependents on the sole condition of performing the duties of vassalage. In the course of time, agriculture, which had been the mainstay of the English race, became necessarily much neglected. Large tracts of land which had formerly been carefully tilled in small holdings were converted in pasturage for sheep, that the grain of foreign countries might be purchased with the wool thus attained. The great mass of the people, however, who were once happy and contented freeholders, now became poverty stricken, widespread famines were frequent, and the lower classes were sometimes obliged to live upon roots and herbs. Little by little this unnatural system of land holding gave way and the old English customs were revived until, with the restoration of Charles II in 1660, the abolition of the tenure of lands by Knight's service removed the last relic of the Feudal System.

It seems strange indeed that, at a time when serfdom was disappearing in the Old World, a powerful company of Dutch merchants in Holland should be planning to introduce all the characteristic features of the system into the New, and the case is rendered all the more remarkable when we remember that the project was conceived three centuries after the hated institution had been cast out from the Netherlands.

Holland, by accident of discovery in 1609, became possessed of the best section of the Atlantic coast. The abundance of fur-bearing animals stimulated the commercial zeal of the Dutch and the merchants of Amsterdam soon had trading posts established at the mouth of the Hudson. A brisk trade sprang up between the Dutch and the Indians, muskets and ammunition finding a ready exchange for good peltries. Not until 1623 did the first party of permanent colonists arrive at Manhattan and very soon cattle, horses, sheep and swine were imported and agriculture had its birth in the New Netherland. Farmers were slow, however, to leave the rich lands of Holland and to encourage permanent homes the West India Company in 1629 issued its famous Charter of Privileges and Exemptions which operated directly to bring on the anti-rent agitation more than two centuries later. A careful study of this charter is of prime importance in connection with the history of the struggle between landlords and tenants which grew out of it. The men of Blenheim Hill began to read it as they discussed the news from Albany County in the winter of 1839-40. Sheldon Peaslee neglected his Latin and Greek for a time that he might become well versed in history. Others, who knew no language save their own, learned the Privileges and Exemptions by heart.

Briefly, the charter offered to any member of the company who should, within four years, bring to New Netherland fifty adults and establish them along the Hudson, a liberal grant of land to be called a manor. The owner, or "patroon," was full proprietor, with exclusive rights, chief magistrate of the manorial courts; in short, lord of the manor.

To secure tenants, settlers were to be exempt from taxation for ten years but they were under bond to stay in one place and develop its resources. The patroon bore the expense of building houses and barns and provided cattle, seeds, and tools. In return for this outlay he received a fixed rent payable in stock or produce and was also entitled to share in the increase of cattle and crops. He might also buy the remainder, for the farmer must not sell to other parties without first offering to the patroon. The tenant must grind his grain at the patroon's mill and had no right to hunt or fish on the estate. There was neither freedom nor dignity in the position of tenant on one of these estates.

In size, the manors might have a frontage on the Hudson of 16 miles, if all on one shore, or eight on both, running back as far as the patroon wished. Such was the beginning of the great estates in eastern New York. The system, somewhat modified, was continued under English rule, which began in 1664. The Blenheim patent was granted to John Weatherhead and others on Nov. 28, 1769. It included a tract of 40,000 acres, nearly square, west of the Schoharie river, its southwest corner being Utsayantha Lake. At the time of the anti-rent war this tract was owned by John A. King, afterward governor of the State.

It is interesting to note, in passing, that the Blenheim Hill community was made up of representatives of the various peoples mentioned in this chapter. The Peaslees and Mayhams are Celtic,—original Briton stock, the former Welch and the latter Caledonians. Clark, Wood, Curtis, Cornell, Kenyon, all are Saxon. Hubbell is Danish. Sage and Champlin are Norman and came with the conqueror into England. Shaver, Vroman, Warner, and Decker all migrated from the Rhine, the last clans to leave the fatherland. Many other families could be included in these divisions. Whatever the line, it was all the same. Back of these men were more than two thousand years of land holding in fee simple. Now that they began to study the problem, looked at in any light, the idea of living upon and improving lands which they could not own began to seem to them atrocious.

CHAPTER VI

The Brimstone Church

ystems of land tenure greatly influence the economic development of a country. Any scheme which perpetuates large estates and makes difficult the growth of small holdings keeps the mass of the agricultural population in a position of dependence. Before the Revolution, great plantations were common in the south while small farms had always been the rule in New England. The Dutch manors in New York developed an aristocracy which was not equalled anywhere else in America. Rensselaerwyck included all the land for a distance of twenty-four miles along both sides of the Hudson and the same distance back into the country on each side. Other great estates were created under English rule and with most of these grants the idea of social station accompanying the possession of land was uppermost. Blenheim was granted sixty-five years after the battle fought in Bavaria during the war of the Spanish succession. John Weatherhead may have been a son of an officer who took part in that famous victory, or connected in some way with the Marlborough family. At the time the patent was issued (1769) probably every acre of the 40,000 was covered with virgin forest. Settlements were not made until some years after the revolution. Many of the first comers were squatters, knowing little and caring less of John Weatherhead, his heirs or assigns. The pioneers were mostly from New England and extremely poor. Land was plenty and capital scarce. Farms could be purchased

Brimstone Meeting House, Blenheim Hill, built in 1815

on long terms of payment or on perpetual leases with an annual rent payable in wheat delivered at Albany. Little consideration was given to land titles at a time when the question of food and shelter overshadowed all others. As the years went on and the land was cleared, the matter of ownership forced itself upon the people. The pioneer with an ax had become the prosperous farmer surrounded by all the property which his industry had won from the soil. Already the perpetual lease was driving families away from Blenheim Hill, westward to the Phelps and Gorham purchase or elsewhere. Men began to feel that after all they were only tenants.

In May, 1840, the Legislature passed an act to provide for the settlement of the anti-rent difficulties. Early in June a meeting was held in the Brimstone church one evening to get at the sentiment of the community, for the Governor had appointed commissioners to confer with tenants and the citizens of the Backbone desired to be heard. Dr. Cornell had proposed the call and nearly every man in the neighborhood responded. They entered the church and took their seats with the same solemnity exhibited at the weekly prayer meeting. It was an unnecessary formality for Thomas Peaslee to call them to order before he explained the purpose of the gathering. For two hours these farmers talked of their grievances, observing the rules of a deliberative body. The speeches were moderate in tone for the most part, although Lyman Root, the one-armed shoemaker, was outspoken against the landlords and hinted at tar and feathers. At length, when no more speakers volunteered, the chairman, fixing his eye upon a man in the audience who had remained silent, said: "There is one here tonight whose words will carry much weight if he will declare himself. It is not the purpose of this meeting to force an expression of opinion from anyone, yet we should know where every man stands." At this there were calls for the man to whom the moderator referred and he slowly arose. He was tall, six feet, of stalwart frame, broad shoulders, a deep chest, a large head, a man of commanding presence. He spoke in a clear deep voice, with the hesitation of a farmer but with the force and earnestness of a statesman.

Mr. Chairman, there is not a man here who does not know where I stand, and, when the crisis comes, every man knows how I will act. Issue will not be joined this year nor next. There has already been too much violence on the part of the anti-renters, and too strong an appeal to arms on the part of the patroons. Justice cannot be secured at the hands of a mob nor can oppression be made permanent under the guise of law and by the aid of the state militia. We cannot question the validity of the patroons' titles, much as we may decry the methods by which they were secured. Such as date back to the Dutch period were provisionally confirmed to the proprietors when the English came in control and so by successive temporary orders until 1685, when a formal grant was issued by the British government through Governor Dongan. In 1704 Queen Anne confirmed the grants and defined the quit-rents to the crown. Finally, the first state constitution, adopted at Kingston in 1777, declared that all grants of land made within the State by the King of Great Britain, or persons acting under his authority, prior to the Revolution, should stand. The title to Rensselaerwyck is as valid as law can make it. The title to Blenheim is likewise so. The terms of our leases can and will be enforced. We can abandon these farms if necessary, and a manor without tenants would be of little use to the landlord. That John A. King came into possession of Blenheim for a valuable consideration and that his title is good are facts which we need not discuss at all, but who cleared this land and whose labor has made it a region of productive farms? Only a generation back, here lay a rough mountain forest. A King on the other side of the Atlantic had conveyed it by deed to a British subject who never cut one tree in the great woods or laid one stone upon another. Men with bare hands came here, men with mouths to feed and backs to warm. The labor of one generation has been expended here. Homes have been built, fields cleared, and the resources of the country developed. Neither the King's hand nor the landlord's did any of this work. My hands have done some of it. Your hands have done much of it. All these years we have been carrying wheat to Albany in payment of rent and the more land we clear the more wheat we carry. Will this payment cease this year, or next year, or the year after? Will this soil that we have dug from under these stones belong to us some day? Go home and read your lease and answer.

Something must be done to change these conditions if we are to prosper as individuals, or if this community is to prosper as a whole. Rent must not be increased. We cannot pay more than we are now paying. Very likely this is also true on other estates, particularly in Albany County where the riots have occurred. I cannot see how anything can come from the law just passed by the Legislature. The landlords have too strong a case at law and the tenants too good a case in equity to effect an easy settlement. In the conflict which is forcing itself upon us, I shall vote and act on the side of the men who have made every rod of this land and who own not a single rod of it.

When the speaker ceased the old church rang with applause and no man present approved the speech more than did the moderator. It gave the anti-renters, however, something to disagree over for Dr. Cornell had contended that the land grants were invalid and probably most of the men present were like minded, yet they saw in the words of the speaker a determination to combat all that was wrong in the system and it was that spirit of resistance after all that made the anti-rent movement formidable.

While the Legislative committee was at work trying to adjust the differences between Stephen Van Rensselaer and his tenants, there was an active discussion of the issue going on among all holders of lease land throughout eastern New York. Nothing ever came directly from the committee's work and the Legislature took no further action in the matter for several years. In the meantime disorder had revived and continued in the western half of the old Rensselaer Manor and spread to the leasehold districts east of the Hudson. Anti-rent societies now sprang up which in time became powerful organizations. They originated, as did the riots, in Albany County, and spread over the whole leasehold district, from Columbia on the east to Delaware on the west.

CHAPTER VII

Platform of the Anti-Rent Society

The first anti-rent society on Blenheim Hill was formed in 1843 and the leading men of the community were enrolled as members. Meetings were held regularly in the Brimstone church, greatly to the disgust of the dominie, who preached against the desecration. The good churchmen, however, from Thomas Peaslee down, all favored the movement. At a well attended meeting held one evening soon after the preliminary organization had been made, John Mayham read the following declaration of principles which may be taken to fairly represent the claims and purposes of the anti-renters.

Platform of the Anti-rent Society.
  I. Unequal taxation is unjust. By the present system the tenants on the Patroon lands are required to pay all taxes on such lands for the support of both county and state. This taxing them for lands owned by somebody else, they hold to be an unjust and exorbitant demand.
  II. The Patroon has full power under the law to collect rent, while the tenant has no power to contest that right. They consider this a great moral wrong.

III. The tenant system has an improper bearing on the elective franchise, through fear of incurring the displeasure of the Patroon.

IV. Tenants are frequently ejected from their farms for non-payment of rent, when there is personal property enough on the premises to pay it.

V. If the tenant, through misfortune, is unable to live up to every requirement of his lease, the same may be forfeited at the will of the landlord.

VI. It may be claimed that the Patroon has these rights under the law and that the tenant has bound himself. Be it replied that the leases were in a manner forced upon all families who now live upon leased premises in manner following: At first, when the country was new, the Patroon was very good and indulgent, to such as would settle on his manor, sometimes giving the use of the land seven years for nothing, with the promise of a good and indulgent lease at the end of that time. During this period considerable improvements were sure to be made upon the land. But now comes the pinch. A lease is made out and the renter sees at once that it is in a considerable degree subversive of his own natural rights as a free citizen. What can he do? He must either accept it, or lose seven years' labor.

VII. We demand the enactment of such laws as will enable the tenants to purchase the land of the Patroons at a fair consideration, and if it be necessary, we call for an amendment to the State Constitution that will forever put an end to the Patroon system.

Dr. Cornell objected to the platform upon the ground that it differed materially from those adopted in the Hudson river counties in that it omitted altogether the vital point at issue, and upon his motion the following plank was proposed in place of the last read:

VII. "The renters hold that the land they occupy is their own, on account of what is called legal possession: that is, being actually on the land, and by enclosing it, while the Patroon's possession is by proxy only. But if it is neither the Patroon's nor the rentees' then they hold that the manor belongs to the State, as they abjure the claims of the pretended owners altogether. Under the idea of statute prohibitions, it is known that men cannot sell their lives, their liberties, their children, their wives, nor their servants. A man cannot burn his own house, nor even abuse a dumb beast, although the animal may be his own. He cannot sell his vote, nor buy one at elections. The statute of prohibition goes against all frauds and usurpations of every nature; on which account it is believed that these leases ought to be shorn of their hateful traits of ancient feudalism, by the shears of legislative authority, and the tenants confirmed in the holding and enjoyment of the farms they now own and occupy."

A heated discussion followed and divided the anti-renters into two factions, one seeing clearly that the law was on the side of the landlord and that it must be changed; the other believing that the landlords had no right, under the law, to the possession of the land. Dr. Cornell went frequently to Catskill, Albany, and other Hudson river towns and he had heard the radical debates that had been held in all that country. He loved right and hated wrong and it angered him to have it allowed that the Patroons held their lands by a clear title. He knew that much property, owned by Tories, had been confiscated after the Revolution, and to his mind the old grants made by the King were null and void. It was not an altogether unreasonable proposition. Many of the best men among the anti-renters believed it thoroughly. Men who had applauded Cornelius Maham when he advanced the opposite view at the first anti-rent meeting held in the Brimstone church came to his house in the days that followed to argue the case with him. But Thomas Peaslee and Thomas Vroman had taken the same view of the case and by the time that Blenheim Hill could boast of an anti-rent society, a clear majority held that way. The platform had been drawn in accordance with this view and the seven planks as presented were, by a close vote, made the official declaration of the society.

"Well," said Dr. Cornell, when the vote was announced, "I want to make one motion that will carry here tonight. I move that at our next meeting we get together in the afternoon and have a pole-raising. I want to see a flag floating here bearing the words: 'Down with the Rent.'"

The motion received a dozen seconds from various parts of the church and was carried with a rush. The tallest and straightest pole that could be found was accordingly raised a week later, just a few rods east of the church on the corner where the cross-road ran north to the Curtis farm. Sixty years after, some workmen repairing the highway at that point came upon the old stump of the famous anti-rent pole, deeply and firmly embedded in the earth. Dr. Cornell saw to it that the defiant flag was kept floating from the pole.

The anti-rent associations which had become general throughout the patroon estates in 1844 included the most moderate and respectable citizens of the counties affected and their action was restricted to perfectly legal measures, such as suits at law, sending representatives to the legislative committees, presenting petitions, publishing matter bearing upon the questions at issue, and making nominations for political offices. The "Indian" bands organized in connection with these associations were composed of the younger and more reckless men who saw in this phase of the movement an opportunity for much of that rough sport which was keenly enjoyed by the yeoman of two generations back. Once under way, the disguise offered a protection under which men committed acts of violence that otherwise would not have been ventured on.

Three tribes of "Indians" were organized among the tenants on the Blenheim patent. The chiefs were Christopher Decker of Blenheim Hill, called Black Hawk; Henry A. Cleveland of Dutch Hill, called Red Jacket; and John McEntyre of Gilboa, called Tecumseh. The principal rendezvous of all three tribes was on the back farm of Thomas S. Peaslee where they frequently assembled for drill and discipline.

The prudence of the three chiefs and the substantial character of the braves prevented any rash acts such as characterized the tribes along the Hudson and in Delaware County. They were bound by strict by-laws, one of which provided that no physical injury should be inflicted on an officer charged with the service of legal papers, and only one instance of actual interference with officers occurred within the territorial limits of the three tribes.

CHAPTER VIII

Fink's Tavern

In the spring of 1844 Gen. John S. Brown, then sheriff of Schoharie County, and Tobias Bouck, under-sheriff, came to the village of North Blenheim armed with what were then called writs of ejectment against a large number of tenants in the towns of Blenheim, Jefferson and Fulton. Arriving in the afternoon they put up at the popular tavern kept by Wm. Fink where they were royally entertained by the proprietor. During the evening several "up-renters," residing on the flats in the vicinity of the village, called to pay their respects and the flowing bowl passed freely. The officers became loud and boastful. Bouck, who was a powerful man in the full vigor of middle life, declared that if interfered with or attacked by "Indians" he would unmask them and lodge them in the county jail. As the evening wore on, the visiting neighbors left the tavern one by one and the two officers settled down to a quiet smoke in front of the blazing hickory logs in the old fashioned fire place.

In the meantime the whole Hill country was astir. No sooner had Brown and Bouck arrived at Blenheim in the afternoon than a fleet runner, Almerin Martin, was dispatched to notify Black Hawk. He sped up the steep mountain side with the swiftness of a deer, reaching the Perry settlement with scarce breath enough to tell the news. Here Stephen Perry caught the message and dashed away to the west, reaching the Decker

Gen. John L. Brown
Sheriff of Schoharie County during the anti-rent war

homestead just in time to intercept Christopher Decker as he was about to set out for the sugar camp. The oxen were immediately left for his sister Sally to unyoke and return to the stable. A lad, Charley Soper, was dispatched into the house for two tin horns. Taking one horn himself, Mr. Decker said to the boy, "Take your horn Charley and run to the hilltop where you can make Bill Champlin hear. Blow till you get an answer. Don't waste any time on Giles Champlin. He is as good as an 'up-renter' already. Now go."

Young Soper knew the meaning of such orders and lost no time. Decker and Perry started immediately through the fields leading to the "camp," blowing the horn at intervals as they ran. Soon the horns were sounding on every side and within an hour from the arrival of Brown and Bouck at the Blenheim Inn, men were starting from the remote settlements on Dutch Hill and Blenheim Ridge, making their way through the snow towards the Peaslee farm.

Two hundred Indians had assembled by nightfall. It was decided, however, that a much smaller force would be sufficient to deal with the sheriff and his deputy and a company of fifty started out under the command of Black Hawk, the others returning to their homes. On their way they met a second messenger who detailed the situation at the tavern. There was no hurry now and the band did not approach the house until after ten in the evening. With all the stealthiness and caution of the native red men and looking not unlike real Indians in their disguise, the anti-renters surrounded the hotel. Having discovered that Brown and Bouck had not yet retired, the band collected in a body, the bar room door opened and in rushed fifty strong men with Black Hawk at their head. Instantly all was confusion. Sheriff Bouck sprang behind the bar, and swinging an axe-handle, threatened to kill any man who dared to approach him. Stephen Perry, a man of phenomenal strength, bounded over the bar and grappled with Bouck. In a fierce struggle Perry wrenched the weapon from the sheriff and threw him bodily over the bar where he was at once seized by a number of braves, thrown upon the floor with great violence and held there until he asked for his release, promising to desist from further resistance. In the meantime Brown had been more easily secured.

At the command of the chief, both men were now brought before him, a considerable space in the room accorded them, and they were permitted to stand free. Addressing them, Black

Hawk said, "Have no fear for your personal safety. Do just as I tell you and no harm will befall you. Remove your slippers."

The sheriffs complied and stood in their stocking feet.

"Put on your boots."

Again they objected. Then addressing the landlord, the chief said:

"Captain Fink, bring these men their overcoats and help them to put them on."

It being evident that the Indians contemplated carrying the officers away from the tavern, Gen. Brown protested.

"Silence!" commanded the chief.

The prisoners were then marched, under strong guard, out of the hotel and placed in a large lumber sleigh with ample protection of robes and blankets. They were then driven up the West Kill road to the saw mill of Fredus Baldwin where the band halted and proceeded to kindle a large fire. The Indians then formed in a large circle around the burning pine stumps, the two prisoners, with Black Hawk and Yellow Jacket (Jesse M. Cornell) within the ring. The chief then gave his orders again.

"Take from your pockets all papers of every description and lay them upon the ground."

Both men now entered a protest and began to speak of the illegal proceedings being enacted.

"Silence!" thundered the chief. Then, to his braves, he said:

"Give the war whoop of your tribe."

A most unearthly yell rent the air and echoed far out in the surrounding forest beyond the shadows of the great light that made every object clearly visible for rods around. The men then took from their pockets several packages of papers and threw them at the chief's feet. Yellow Jacket gathered them up and examined them carefully. All such as related to the collection of rents were, by the order of the chief, thrown into the fire. This being accomplished, a second blood-curdling war-whoop burst upon the night and several Indians called out, "Tar and feather them." There were among the young braves some of the greatest dare-devils in the country, Stephen and Tom Curtis, Bill Vroman, the Cornell boys,—fine, manly fellows, all of them, but bound to have fun and absolutely fearless. The boastings of Bouck had made them anxious to apply the tar and a goodly supply had been provided. The two officers would have received harsh treatment had not Sheldon Peaslee stepped forward with a characteristic speech:

> We have gone far enough tonight. These men have complied with your demands and should be released. Might does not make right. They have atoned for their boasting. They have discovered that the men of Blenheim Hill are not afraid of them and that we have here a score who can handle them singly. They have promised to serve no more papers and to keep away from us in the future. That is all we want. Take them back to the tavern now and let them go.

Not a voice was raised to oppose these earnest words and the sheriffs were escorted to the sleigh and returned to Fink's hotel, where they arrived before daybreak.

The scene of this incident is the most lonely spot in the town. At that time Fredus Baldwin owned 1800 acres. He, with two brothers, came from Tennessee. Rachel, the wife of Fredus, was an "up-renter," believing in obeying and upholding the laws of the country. Her husband and sons were anti-rent sympathizers. She persisted in blowing her ram's horn at meal time in spite of the protests of the Indians. That ram's horn is now preserved at the Old Stone Fort at Schoharie. The next morning after the Indians' visit this lady discovered the foot prints, the smouldering fire, and the discarded tar-bucket. Her imagination did not rest and she read the male members of her family a lecture on law and order which would have done credit to a patroon.

This bold, high-handed, forcible and organized resistance to the officers of the law produced a profound sensation on Blenheim Hill, in Schoharie County, and throughout the state, for Sheriff Brown reported the whole proceeding to the Governor and the affair was widely heralded. Up to this time the anti-rent party had, to all outward appearances, been fairly well united, although the speech of Cornelius Maham at the first public meeting in the Brimstone church had started a faction admitting that the rents were legal and opposed to violating the law in any way. Some of these men, though they attended the anti-rent meetings and were identified with the organization, were opposed to its methods. They had not taken to wearing disguises and, in consequence, were called "up-renters." The time came, during the following year, when they manifested a strong fighting spirit themselves, but now they were loud in denouncing the "outrage" as they called the night's work on the West Kill.

CHAPTER IX

The Great Summit Meeting

The contention over the capture of Brown and Bouck became so strong that a public meeting was called to assemble on Blenheim Ridge. The date fixed was at the time of a general training and the meeting was held in the open air on the "green." A large platform had been erected near the road at the foot of the slope. Red Jacket, who was a good orator, spoke at length, counseling moderation. The principal address was made by "The Prophet," an agitator from Columbia County, of whom more will be heard later. Thos. Peaslee took the platform and called upon his listeners to live within the law. He was followed by Lyman Root who advised less moderation and more resistance, evidently to the liking of the crowd, for he was greeted with a deafening war whoop when he closed. The excitement was becoming intense. Wm. Maham made his way to the platform and waved his hand for silence. The tumult ceased and he began to speak. He had not proceeded far when it became evident that the anti-renters were not in a mood to hear his radical denunciation of the practice of wearing a disguise. Their attitude nerved him to still fiercer speech and he declared, "Any man who wears a mask is a coward."

Instantly a hundred guns were leveled at him. Stepping to the front of the platform he stripped open his homespun shirt and exposed his bare breast.

"Here is my heart. Shoot if you dare! I repeat that any man who wears a disguise is a coward."

The climax had been reached. Not a shot was fired and the guns dropped.

This meeting on the Ridge was a small affair compared with the great gathering that assembled two weeks later at Summit when 1500 "Indians" were present and as many more anti-rent sympathizers who did not wear a disguise. It was the largest anti-rent meeting ever held in Schoharie County and one of the largest in the State. The three Blenheim tribes were present to a man and Henry A. Cleveland made a stirring address. The whole temper of the crowd was belligerent, reflecting, to a large extent, the temper of the community.

There had been friction between officers and citizens at Summit from the beginning of the agitation. Geo. H. Ferguson acted as a signal man for the anti-renters. Whenever a constable or sheriff appeared, Ferguson would go to the east window of his shop, located in Lake's store, and blow a blast upon his bugle. In a few minutes horns were tooting on every side and within half an hour Indians could be seen popping out of the woods in every direction. If the officers attempted to serve any papers they were immediately driven away from the locality, the Indians sometimes following them for miles until they were well on their way back to Schoharie. If the officers proceeded too slowly, their speed would be increased by the whistle of bullets about their heads.

The day of the Summit meeting was chosen by the sheriff and his deputies to visit the town, keeping well away from the Four Corners, however. The officers encountered John F. Sawyer dressed as an Indian and riding alone on his way to the village. A fight ensued in which Sawyer was shot in the hand, losing two fingers. He finally took refuge in a house but the officers located him. He jumped through a window and made his way to the residence of one Harvey Boughton where he secreted himself several days. Sawyer was afterward elected sheriff of Schoharie County.

Not long after the Summit meeting, another was held at Morseville in the town of Jefferson. Here eighty yoke of cattle were driven in, each bringing a load of anti-renters. Great preparations were made for this meeting, flags and banners were everywhere displayed, and great enthusiasm prevailed. The Indians were out in full disguise. The Allan boys of Summit made many false faces and bright dresses. The Franklin brothers of South Jefferson were present and sang many anti-rent songs of their own composition. They attended all these gatherings far and near, and their songs were very popular. One of them ran like this:

> The moon was shining silver bright,
> The sheriff came at dead of night,
> High on a hill an Indian true,
> And on his horn this blast he blew, —
>
> Chorus:
> Get out of the way, big Bill Snyder,
> We'll tar you coat and feather your hide, sir.
>
> Bill ran and ran till he reached the wood,
> And then with horror still he stood,
> For he saw an Indian tall and grim,
> And heard a tin horn not a rod from him.
>
> Chorus.
>
> Bill thought he heard the sound of a gun,
> He cried in fright, "Oh my race is run!
> Better that I had never been born
> Than come within sound of that big horn."
>
> Chorus.

Next day the body of Bill was found,
His writs were scattered all over the ground,
And by his side a jug of rum,
Told how Bill to his end had come.

Chorus.

The anti-rent agitation now spread westward into Delaware County, the first public meeting being held at Roxbury with headquarters at the public house kept by Thomas Keater. Several Blenheim Hill Indians attended in full uniform and a number of the younger men of Roxbury put on the disguise for the first time that day. The first open act of hostility was perpetrated soon after this meeting, on July 6, upon the premises of John B. Gould who had incurred the displeasure of the Indians by refusing to desist from blowing a horn as a signal to call his workmen to dinner. That day Mr. Gould, as usual, blew his horn at noon when five Indians, armed for fight, presented themselves at his door and demanded that he obey the authority of the anti-rent association. An angry discussion ensued and the Indians left. On the following Tuesday they appeared again. The story of what followed is graphically told by Jay Gould in his *History of Delaware County:*

The sun had just arrived at the meridian, when a favorable opportunity presenting itself, the signal whoop was given, and the savage horde sprang from their hiding places, and with demonlike yells rushed up and surrounded Mr. Gould, who was standing with his little son in front of the house. We were that son, and how bright a picture is still retained upon the memory, of the frightful appearance they presented as they surrounded that parent with fifteen guns pointed within a few feet of his head, while the chief stood over him with fierce gesticulations, and sword drawn. Oh, the agony of my youthful mind, as I expected every moment to behold him prostrated a lifeless corpse upon the ground. His doting care and parental love had endeared him to his family. But he stood his ground firmly; he never yielded an inch. Conscious of right, he shrank from no sense of fear, and finally, when a few neighbors had gathered together, a second time they were driven from the premises without the accomplishment of their object. The Indians marched off the premises and down the road in single file. About three miles below they overtook and tarred and feathered Hiram More.

About this time bands of Indians several times assaulted the sheriff of Columbia County, took his papers from him and burned them and finally they were held responsible for two murders at Smoky Hollow, a little place about six miles from Hudson. Two chiefs, "Big Thunder" and "Little Thunder," were arrested and lodged in jail. A movement on the part of the anti-renters to rescue these prisoners led to the calling out of the militia by Governor Bouck which prevented any outbreak. The general excitement throughout the Patroon district became intense, and the most bitter feeling existed between the up-renters and the Indians everywhere.

CHAPTER X

"Down with the Rent!"

On the 10th of August a large anti-rent meeting was held at West Sand Lake. A fortnight later Joseph Perry and Randall Clark discussed the account of this gathering as printed in the Albany Atlas while a heavy thunder shower had driven them from the harvest field.

"Gov. Bouck is really on the side of the tenants," said Mr. Perry.

"Bouck is a politician," replied Mr. Clark who was too strong a Whig to admit virtue in a Democrat. "He has done no more than Seward did. The anti-rent vote will do him little good this fall anyway, my way of thinking, for the Barnburners are likely to control the state convention and if they do Silas Wright will be the Democratic candidate."

"Gov. Bouck is a shrewd man," Mr. Perry answered, "and I would like to see him nominated again. He did not damage his case any at West Sand Lake the other day."

The conference to which Joseph Perry referred was the most important one held that year and in the old files of the Atlas may be found the following account from a correspondent.

"West Sand Lake, Aug. 10, 1844.
Editor of the Atlas:—It having been generally understood that Gov. Bouck was to visit us today, in accordance with an arrangement with a committee of the tenants,

Gov. William C. Bouck
Schoharie County's only governor

there was according a large turnout of probably some 2000 of the tenantry. A flag was raised, having on it the representation of an Indian with the motto—

DOWN WITH THE RENT

And in one of the windows of a tavern was placed a transparency representing another "native" with the motto—"The land is mine saith the Lord."

About 150 of the celebrated though anomalous tribe of Indians who have been the instrument of all the trouble, were also in attendance. These savages presented a most comical and grotesque appearance, and certainly looked anything but ferocious, or ferociously inclined. They wore

masks, in most cased of glazed muslin, with apertures for
sight and breathing, covering the head and neck entirely,
and blouses of calico, decorated with colored patches,
furs, etc., and from their ears hung large brass rings, while
a few had strings of beads hanging from their noses. The
chiefs, as they were termed, were more profusely decorated, and by way of distinction bore long spears. They
were variously armed, some carrying swords, knives, bits
of scythes, and threatening-looking cheese knives, others
clubs and muskets, while all had pistols in their belts. The
language spoken was our common vernacular, mouthed
with a strange intonation, with an occasional sprinkle of
Dutch. "Natives," was the term applied by their chiefs in
addressing them, although they were probably divided
into several tribes as I heard one leader designated as the
"Tuscarora chief."

About half past ten o'clock the approach of the executive of the State was announced by discharges of a cannon.
His excellency was escorted by a committee to the house
of Burton A. Thomas, where the conference were waiting
for him.

The Indians, during the conference which lasted two or
three hours, retired to the woods, the people in the meanwhile in the village gathering into knots discussing anti-
rent matters and the probable result of the conference.

At about 2 o'clock the Governor and committee retired
to dinner, when the church bell was rung, and the people
assembled in front of the church. Mr. Gregorys, one of the
committee of conference, then mounted the stand and addressed them. He detailed the particulars of the interview
with Gov. Bouck. He stated that he had proposed to the
Governor that the question as to the title should be left to
the Governors of any three of the New England states
(Connecticut excepted) for their examination and decision.

To this Governor Bouck demurred for the reason that they were common men like himself, with one exception, that of Gov. Briggs of Massachusetts, who was a lawyer, and therefore were not a whit more competent to decide. He also said that the Governor had informed them that he directed the sheriff of the county not to serve any process without consulting the Attorney General and the Justice of the Supreme Court. He concluded with an earnest exhortation to stand firm on the ground they had taken, and continue to resist any attempt to enforce the payment of their rents by all possible means. No matter what is done, he said, they must refuse the payment of rent, and must rely on their arms—the arms of the law, which was as much on their side as on that of the opponents. The orator added that he was informed the Attorney General had given it as his opinion that the sheriff had not exerted his entire power vested in him, and that until he had done so, the State Executive could do nothing in the matter.

When the speaker had concluded, the Indians came galloping furiously into the village under another discharge from the six-pounder. One of them was unfortunately thrown from his horse, and trampled upon by those who followed. Upon picking him up he was found to be much injured and he was carried into a neighboring house, where he died about an hour after. His name was Goss.

While the Indians were attending to their wounded comrade, the Governor was escorted to the church where he was greeted. While engaged in shaking hands with the people the Indians formed in a circle surrounding the Governor and people. This was against the express wishes of the Governor and upon the chief manifesting a desire to greet him he immediately left the ground. The Indians then dispersed, as did most of the people, and the Governor left for Albany.

Harvest was not over when news came from Roxbury that Timothy Corbin had been tarred and feathered on general training day while assisting the sheriff in the service of official papers. The sheriff's papers were also taken and destroyed. There were those among the Blenheim Hill Indians who were anxiously waiting to go on the war path again. The tales that came in from other localities filled them with restlessness. An opportunity soon presented itself.

Tobias Houghtailing, a constable living on the Ridge, had made himself very obnoxious by serving papers for Colbia Reed and it was decided to capture him. About twenty of the younger braves set out one morning in full disguise. They stopped at the home of Giles Champlin on the way and demanded a bucket of tar, which was refused.

"Don't waste any words with him," said one Indian to his companions, "I know where the tar bucket is and will get it myself. If he interferes we'll give him some of it."

The tar was secured and the Indians moved on. They did not find the constable and towards evening started for home. A halt was made, however, and the band stole back after nightfall. They found Houghtailing and marched him out near the Ruliffson homestead. There the chief put it to vote whether they should tar and feather the officer. All in favor were to pass over to the right side of the road. Two stalwart Indians pulled Houghtailing over on the right side, whereupon the chief declared that the vote was unanimous and the coat of tar and feathers was applied accordingly.

"Tell Colbia Reed that Giles Champlin paid for the tar," said one of the Indians as they released the constable, but that dignitary was too much interested in his own escape to heed the command. A gauntlet had been suggested while the coat was being given and the Indians arranged themselves in two lines but the sight of the officer provoked so much laughter that not a club was raised as he shot through the center and disappeared in the darkness.

CHAPTER XI

Riot

I t would be a matter of absorbing interest to go into State
and National politics in 1844 as the men of Blenheim Hill
saw and understood the issue, but the story is too long. The
Whigs nominated Clay for President in May at Baltimore and
Van Buren expected the Democrats to nominate him later in the
month in the same city. He had a majority of the delegates but
could not gain the required two-thirds, and Polk was nominated.
There were many "Hunkers" among the Democrats on Blenheim Hill, men who followed Van Buren and opposed the an-
nexation of Texas. The State convention was held September 4,
and the "Barnburners" defeated the anti-Texas men and nominated Silas Wright for governor. The Whigs nominated Filmore
on September 11. The Schoharie County Anti-Rent convention
was held at Peter A. Borst's in Fulton on Wednesday, September
25. Seven out of the twelve towns in the county were represented.
James Griffin of Middleburgh was chairman of the convention
and Thomas Ferguson of Summit, secretary. Blenheim supported Thomas Peaslee for the nomination for Member of Assembly. Henry Tibbits and Seymour Boughton were nominated
for Members, Schoharie at that time having two representatives
in the Assembly.

Snow came early on Blenheim Hill in the autumn of 1844.
The ground was white in the last days of September. Not
only was the season thus cut short but crops had not been up

The Ridge Street, now known as South Gilboa Road
Scene of exciting incidents in anti-rent days

to average and now, as the farmers commenced to dig their potatoes, they found them almost a total failure. An old copy of the Schoharie Republican says: "Farmers of this county will suffer greatly from the disease or rot of the potatoes. Some fields are not worth digging—others yield a half a crop, and occasionally a field that is but very little injured. The disease prevails extensively."

An Albany Argus of the same date says:

We understand that this disease has extended into the towns of this county, particularly in the Helderberg region. The most extraordinary circumstance about the rot is, that there is no telling the cause. The finest looking fields are suddenly and at once stricken down; and it is therefore supposed that an insect stings the top of the potato plant and thus infuses the poison into the seed.

Blenheim Hill home of John A. Clark in anti-rent times

Wheat had already commenced to fail on Blenheim Hill, and now the loss of the potato crop proved a serious blow to the farmers and the burden of rent day was brought home to them as never before. A short hay crop with snow in September made the outlook still more dubious. There was talk of "going west" and an exodus began which lasted for a decade and took from the Backbone some of its best blood. The route lay first to Cattaraugus County and finally extended to Wisconsin.

The election in 1844 came on. Silas Wright was chosen governor by 10,000 votes; Polk carried New York and was elected President. Clay lost the Anti-Rent vote in New York and with it lost the presidency. The Anti-Rent party carried seven counties. In his first message to the legislature, Gov. Wright discussed the anti-rent movement and the disorders that occurred. Early in the session of the Legislature, on Jan. 25, 1845, an act was passed to prevent persons appearing disguised and armed and, being approved by the Governor, became a law. It was directed at the anti-rent Indians and intended to break up that part of the organization.

While this bill was being discussed and before it became a law, a largely attended and very representative anti-rent meeting was held at Berne, Albany County, on January 15. John Mayham was present as a delegate from Blenheim and made one of the principal speeches. Resolutions were passed calling upon all anti-renters to stand together politically but condemning acts of lawlessness. A report of the meeting and copy of the resolutions were carried to Albany in the hope that the Legislature would not pass the proposed bill, for it was felt that such a law would arouse the anger of the extreme wing of the anti-rent party. This is just what happened.

The first violation of the new law to receive attention came in a few days in the town of Roxbury. The Delaware County grand jury found an indictment against D. W. Squires and an order for his arrest was placed in the hands of under-sheriff Osman N. Steele, who proceeded to Roxbury on February 11 and, in conformity with the new law, warned out a sufficient number of persons to co-operate with him in the performance of his duty. The sheriff and his party arrived at the Squires house in the middle of the night, forced an entrance, and found the object of their search concealed between the straw-tick and feather-bed on which his wife and his mother were sleeping.

Squires was arrested and taken to the Delhi jail the next day. It was reported that he was engaged in tarring Corbin during the previous summer and forcibly taking the papers from Sheriff More at the same time. Anticipating trouble, the sheriff ordered Captain North to proceed to Delhi with his company and hold themselves in readiness to obey orders. On the afternoon of the 13th, companies had arrived from Franklin, Meredith and Walton.

The arrest of Mr. Squires, who was the chief "Big Thunder" among the Indians, created intense excitement. The sheriff thought it prudent not to call out any more companies, for those from the three towns named were the only ones in Delaware County in which the anti-renters were not in the majority. No attempt was made to free Big Thunder and nothing further worthy of note occurred until March 11, when under-sheriff Steele was himself captured and held a prisoner at Andes, a village about ten miles from Delhi.

Steele was able to dispatch a messenger to Delhi who eluded the Indians and carried the following letter:

Andes, March 11, 1845

To the Sheriff: Sir, — We left Andes yesterday about five o'clock, for Delhi, but were stopped on the road, and compelled to return to this place. We are now at Hunting's. The house is now surrounded by men in disguise, about one hundred strong. They intend, as near as I can ascertain, to take my papers, tar and feather me, and pass me over to the Middletown tribe. I shall never be able to reach home unless you come over with all the force you can raise. Let every man come armed, and determined to do his duty or die on the spot. Lose no time but get here as soon as possible.

Yours,

O. W. STEELE

9 o'clock A.M.

Steele and another officer, Charles Parker, took refuge in the garret, where, being well armed, they were enabled to keep the Indians at bay. The messenger with all possible speed hastened to Delhi where Steele's letter was made public by the sheriff. Steps were at once taken to send relief and in an incredibly short time the sheriff and his posse were marching through the snow, slush and mud from Delhi to Andes. It was a motley array— lawyers, physicians, merchants, tradesmen, mechanics, and citizens, on foot, on horseback, in carriages, and all well armed with almost every conceivable weapon of war. As they neared Andes the news of their coming was carried in advance of them and the Indians quickly dispersed, leaving Steele and Edgerton unharmed, though they gladly welcomed the rescuing party and accompanied them back to Delhi.

News of this affair reached the Head-of-the-river on the evening of the 11th and was carried to Blenheim Hill the following day.

"By hokey-nettie," said Jacob Shaver, when he heard the story, "if the posse ever comes here we'll give 'em tar, every durn man of 'em."

"They might catch you Jake, and put you in jail," said his wife Lucretia.

"I guess not by hokey-nettie, Lettie. I can outrun all the durn horses they can get together. Besides, if Bill Vroman, and Steve Perry and Tom Curtis should ever get after 'em, all the rest of us would have to do would be to rub on the tar and stick on the feathers."

The time came, that summer, when Jacob Shaver found it necessary to match his speed against the posse's swiftest horses.

CHAPTER XII

A Divided House

The exciting news from Delaware County caused the citizens of Blenheim Hill to hold a meeting of special importance at the Brimstone church within a few days. Further trouble was expected in Roxbury and at other points over the county line and many of the more conservative men felt that the Blenheim Hill Indians ought not to be connected with the disorders. The radicals, however, openly sympathized with the Delaware Indians and were anxious to help them, while a few "up-renters" were growing bolder in denouncing the whole Indian movement. It was expected that the meeting would be a stormy one and so it proved. It was preceded by a monster parade of Indians dressed in calico and disguised with leather faces. There were a number of "up-renters" present, men who took the part of the landlords openly, or, in a few instances, those who passed as neutral but reported to the landlords every movement of their anti-rent neighbors. The "up-renters" called themselves the law and order party while the Indians used the shorter name of Tory to designate all such. The epithet of Tory on the one hand and "outlaw" on the other passed freely at the meeting. Men of the law and order faction who denounced the Indians, however, had only to wait until the following summer to witness a drunken posse ride through their fields of standing grain, throw their fences down, shoot their neighbors, and insult their wives and daughters in their own homes.

One of the first speakers at the meeting was Amos Loper who lived over on the Ridge. Tradition has preserved the following extracts from his address:

> The anti-renters in all parts of the various manors are growing stronger and becoming more united. There must be a remedy for these evils or else our government is not based upon just principles. Here almost the entire community must suffer from the avarice and cupidity of a few land aristocrats with a very doubtful tenure to the land they claim. This remnant of Feudalism will never grow less troublesome and the sooner the true remedy is applied, the better. I say, "down with the rent," and the way to win is to resist payment and to resist all attempts at collecting rents. It is open robbery to allow the continuance of manorism. Talk about law and order! The law is on our side and so is most of the order and so it will continue.

Thomas Peaslee did not have to be urged to take the floor, nor was his voice strange to the old Brimstone church. He said:

> I am proud to boast that this community is united, almost as one man, in dispelling the dark and demoralizing influence of these legalized and judicial robbers. I believe the day is almost at hand when constitutional rights will be equally enjoyed by all men. Honest men, men with pure motives, are in this anti-rent movement. It is the solemn and imperative duty of every true patriot, of every man who loves his country, who loves truth and justice and human rights, to come forward and help put down this miserable clique of landlords who live by robbing the yeomanry of our country. The people are sovereign here and we intend to use the means and secure the power which the Constitution and God Almighty have granted us.

Peaslee Homestead

Benjamin P. Curtis followed Thomas Peaslee, as he often did in prayer meeting. At the outset he had told his neighbors that he must take time to pray over the matter before he could take part in such a conflict. He evidently prayed to good purpose, for he was a loyal supporter of the anti-renters and his oldest boys were leaders in the Indian bands. He spoke earnestly, with deliberation, and with telling effect:

How comes it that the landlords are entitled to this land? Suppose there were some sort of contracts entered into a half century or more ago. In the course of events and by natural changes they have become void. They are not now what were agreed upon at all. When the old wheat rents were made no one thought that the land would refuse to raise wheat after a term of years. Suppose it had been a potato rent. Would it have been fair to have given a fixed number of bushels last fall when the potatoes all rotted in the field? The terms of the contract should change with the season. Let me remind you too, how the tenants are treated. The sheriffs of the various counties call out a set of bullies who march about the country, arrest men and drag them to jail without knowing or caring whether they are guilty or innocent. It is no longer safe for a farmer to go to Albany or to show himself in any of the larger towns where the patroons control the officers of the law. Let us show the landlords that we are united and determined to have our rights, asking nothing but what is our due.

The more pertinent questions of wearing disguises, suppressing the blowing of horns, and the use of tar and feathers were not touched upon by those speakers, such matters being reserved for the wigwam councils that were held in a little clearing in the woods west of Sheldon Peaslee's residence on the lands of Dr. Hilton on the site of an old charcoal pit made by Dick Hilton. There were up-renters present, however, who started a discussion of these subjects and Giles Champlin attempted to advocate the allowing of dinner horns to be blown as formerly, showing that it was a great inconvenience to many not to be allowed to use the horns in calling men to meals. He was interrupted by some one calling out, "Colbia Reed pats you on the back and you talk like a Tory for him," to which the speaker retorted, "I pay my rent and obey the law. I have a right to blow a horn—" but cries of "Tory," "One of Colbia Reed's Tories," and "Down with the rent," discouraged the speaker and he sat down. The facts were that Giles Champlin was prospering in a small way in spite of the land system. He was religiously prompt in the payment of rent and in meeting other obligations and Colbia Reed had befriended him time and again. The monied man of the town admired the growing young farmer who in turn respected and venerated the landlord. But when this tenant attempted to say anything in favor of a patroon at an anti-rent meeting he brought down upon himself the wrath of his neighbors. While he was called an "up-renter," no one ever accused him of being an "informer." He would not have acted in harmony with some of the men who made up the Blenheim Hill tribe of Indians in any event for his Norman blood had lost none of its combativeness, and perhaps that was one reason why he opposed their acts. He stood loyally with the tenants when it came to voting and even opposed Colbia Reed in politics.

There were other speakers at the meeting, the general temper of which was stoutly opposed to landlordism, even to the extent of upholding the Delaware tribes in their recent work. A report of the gathering, and the tone of the speeches, reached Delhi and Schoharie and was also reported in Columbia County when Dr. Cornell next rode his cream colored nag over the river to see his many patients there. "Old News Carrier" the landlords called him and he rather enjoyed the distinction for he was heart and soul in the anti-rent cause.

Some of the tenants on Blenheim Hill were cautious and not always firm in their support of the movement. Lyman Root's loyalty was sometimes questioned, though he was probably true to the Indians. James K. Porn was an "up-renter" who always kept his wits about him whenever a stranger appeared, prepared to talk on either side as the case might demand. He owned a little patch of ground by no means the best on the Backbone. On the day following the meeting he was at work alone on his land when two travelers came along and engaged him in conversation. The landscape at that place was not promising and James' humble cottage did not bespeak prosperity.

"Do you own this farm?" one of the strangers asked.

"No," replied the shrewd yeoman who knew that even his law and order principles would not save him if they were officers, "I am not such a — — fool as you think."

CHAPTER XIII

The Wigwam

The anti-renters of Dutch Hill were frequently at the wigwam of the Blenheim Hill Indians although they had a camping ground of their own about three quarters of a mile north of Eminence village on lands of the Harders, not far from where four towns corner. Red Jacket was a famous chief whose identity baffled the officers, for the character was assumed by both Henry Cleveland and Jesse M. Cornell. Among the braves were the Plosses, Harders, Felters, and Tompkins. These men were all present at the camp on the Hilton farm when the next news from Roxbury was discussed.

Early on the morning of March 14, deputy sheriff Steele and E. S. Edgerton started by different routes from Delhi to Roxbury to make arrests as that town was considered the most turbulent part of the anti-rent district in Delaware County. Upon reaching the village a party of one hundred and thirty Indians, well armed, was discovered and immediately charged upon by the officers who had with them a mounted posse numbering forty men. A skirmish ensued during which shots were exchanged but the Indians were routed and fled to the woods, eight of the number being captured in a hard hand-to-hand fight. One of the prisoners proved to be a constable of the town. The party now started for Delhi, picking up four more prisoners at Bloomville and lodging all in the county jail. That night horns could be heard in every direction among the mountains about Delhi and a large number of Indians assembled, but the jail was strongly guarded and no attempt was made to rescue the prisoners, four of whom, Burrill, Tompkins, Osterhout, and Knapp, were subsequently convicted and sentenced to Sing Sing for two years, but all were pardoned by Gov. Wright before the expiration of their terms.

The news of the Roxbury raid added fuel to the flame, not only in that town but throughout the disturbed districts. Events were rapidly approaching a crisis which each side felt would be decisive. There came days and weeks and even months of waiting, however, before Law and Right met in mortal combat.

School began in May at the little school-house west of the Brimstone church. The boys on their way to and from school saluted the anti-rent flag that still waved from the liberty pole on the corner east of the church. One morning a second pole, about twenty feet high, appeared near the first and nailed to the top of it was a board on which was painted a British flag. It had been placed there by Sam Root, a notorious Tory, who lived with his brother, Lyman P. Root, the shoemaker, and his wife, Mary Ann. The sight of this hated emblem was more than young America could stand. Among the youngsters were Isaac Peaslee, the Warner boys, the Curtis boys, and others who usually met on the turn of the road. They pelted the flag with stones and knocked it down. Sam replaced it a few times but the boys lost no time tearing it away and the old anti-rent flag finally waved alone again.

During the same month over in Columbia County the sheriff, while walking along the road with two assistants upon his return from executing a writ of possession, was deliberately fired upon from the cover of some bushes near the road, and himself and one of his assistants severely (though not dangerously) wounded. The perpetrators of this assault were never discovered.

On the 4th of June, John Allen, the agent of Charlotte D. Verplanck, obtained of Justice Peter P. Wright a warrant for the arrest

A Blenheim Hill meadow

of Moses Earle of Andes, against whom a debt of $64 was claimed as arrears of rent. A levy was made and the sale attempted, but as the neighbors and other attendants of the sale seemed to have made an agreement not to bid on any of the property, in fact, to "boycott" the sheriff, the sale was finally postponed to one o'clock in the afternoon of the seventh of August.

All through the summer the coming sale on the Earle farm was earnestly discussed. Under-sheriff Steele had become the object of special hatred on the part of the anti-renters as he had been prominent in the whole course of the difficulties and was instrumental in causing the greater number of the arrests, being much more aggressive than Sheriff More. It was expected that many Indians would attend the sale, not only from the various towns in Delaware County, but from adjoining counties as well. Many a housewife on Blenheim Hill plied the needle diligently in making a calico dress for some one or more members of her

A Blenheim Hill scene

family to be worn as a disguise when the various tribes should gather at Andes. The matter was gone over carefully at more than one wigwam meeting in the Hilton woods and men could be seen crossing the fields in every direction at nightfall, making their way to the camp for drill and consultation. The officers were informed of these preparations and determined to start a counter action, Sheriff More of Delaware acting with Sheriff John S. Brown of Schoharie in this matter. These officers believing that the most formidable band of Indians would hail from Blenheim Hill, it was determined to invade the Backbone with strong forces a few days before the sale and arrest Dr. John Cornell, B. P. Curtis, and Thomas Peaslee, who had come to be regarded as the most active anti-renters who supported the Indians in that community. If these men could be secured it was thought that the tribe would very likely make no effort to send help to Andes, especially if a strong force should be assembled to effect the capture of "Old News Carrier," Ben Curtis and the "Old Chief," as the three Blenheim Hill worthies were known to the officers and the landlords. Sheriff Brown was anxious to visit the neighborhood again at the head of a posse for he still smarted under the disgrace at Baldwin's mill. It was arranged to start a posse on the morning of August 4 from Gilboa, and Broome Center, while a third company was to proceed up the Schoharie valley, picking up recruits on the road. The several detachments were on their way early but the tin horns heralded their coming. From house to house up and down the Schoharie valley the horns blew until they echoed over the Mine Kill and encircled Blenheim Hill. The farmers knew that something un-usual was happening or about to happen; just what they could not tell. They sent the shrill message on, however, and early got responses from Dutch Hill, the answering horns being heard over the Neuterbark.

The general alarm purported ill and the men hurried to the camping ground, awaiting the arrival of some runner who should give definite information. Meanwhile the invading forces came on through the hot August sun and toiled up the steep mountain sides leading to the Backbone's summit. The posse for the most part was composed of landlords, their sons, dependents, and hirelings, though some had been impressed with no liking for the work in hand. Before the first division reached the Hill, messengers had brought in a full report of their coming so that the tenants understood their danger and were prepared to meet it.

CHAPTER XIV

"Run, the Posse Is Coming!"

Sheriff Brown and Under-sheriff Bouck had started from Schoharie late on Sunday afternoon and made their way up the Schoharie valley by moonlight, increasing their posse by impressment as they proceeded. A watch was kept out down along the rocks below Blenheim and they approached the narrows with fear and trembling. Every rock and tree and shrub assumed the form of some stalwart Indian and many a sturdy Dutchman was in momentary fear of being shot. Four lumber wagons conveyed the well armed band of citizens under command of the sheriff. When they reached Blenheim village it was midnight. Almerin Martin, a youth of nineteen, had met them at the foot of the bear's ladder and hastened on ahead to conceal himself in the burying ground above the rocks in the lower village. He stood with one hand on a tombstone as the wagons halted in the road below, and heard the sheriff order out a guard. The hair on the young man's head fairly lifted his hat and he concluded it was high time to get away. Keeping well up above the rocks and following a path that he knew, he hastened with all possible speed to the upper village and aroused Freegift P. Martin who carried the news to Alvin Martin at the old tollgate on the Jefferson road. Alvin ran up Darling Hollow to Charles Goodenough's. In the meantime horns aroused alike the anti-renters and the posse and as the latter advanced some were praying, some were swearing, and others singing, according as each thought would be the most effective way to keep off an Indian attack. When the teams had advanced a very little ways above the upper village the men refused to go further that night and compelled the sheriff to return to Fink's tavern where they thought they would be comparatively safe until morning.

When the start was made the next morning as many as could do so procured horses. They were met at the foot of Blenheim Hill by a mounted posse from Gilboa. No sooner had they left the valley than an Indian scout kindled a signal fire along the banks of the Schoharie at a spot where the same could be seen from a few rods from John Mayham's log house where he kept a boy watching. The message having been thus quickly sent and received, it was in like manner carried forward to the camp in the Hilton woods as well as to Dutch Hill and points beyond.

Coming up the valley from that direction, John Mayham's residence was reached first. In the meadow back of the house a halt was made and a plan of action decided upon. The place was searched but no men could be found. On the opposite side hill where stood one of the barns, a long ways from the house, a man was seen to come out of a door and make for the woods. It was Stephen Mayham, a brother of John. Several of the posse fired at the retreating Indian but the distance was so great that he was not shot.

Having thus commenced hostilities, it was decided to leave the horses for the present and proceed in solid column to the residence of Thomas Peaslee, a half mile above, whose capture was greatly desired by the officers. Just beyond the log house, John Mayham had sixteen acres of standing rye, all ready for the harvest. Into this field the posse turned their horses to trample down and destroy the grain and the sixty animals thus let loose accomplished the work during the day. It was the beginning of a fortnight's work of lawlessness on the part of the men claiming to be in the service of the State, the beginning of a reign of terror on Blenheim Hill.

From John Mayham's the posse proceeded up the course of a little stream to the home of Sheldon Peaslee. It will be recalled that their coming had been heralded early in the morning and a council called. It was decided to begin drawing rye from the back side hill, keeping a watchman out. Accordingly, the oxen were yoked and hitched to the wagon and the men proceeded to the field. The rye was in shock. There were thirteen acres, surrounded on three sides by a heavy growth of timber. Sheldon Peaslee did picket duty himself that morning. Among the men at work in the field were Smith Peaslee, E. Babcock, William Clark, D. W. Griggs, Jule Conklin, John Warner, and Charles Scudder. Isaac Peaslee, a little lad of seven, was with the men to ride the old mare Sal, hitched ahead of the oxen. One load had been put on the wagon and all were ready to go to the barn when the watch called out:

"Run, the posse is coming."

The men all started for the woods excepting Smith Peaslee, who remained to take the oxen from the wagon and chain them to a stump and help Ike on the old mare and start him for the barn. The little lad had proceeded up the steep hillside towards home only a few hundred yards when he met the posse, armed to the teeth. They immediately stopped him and asked for information concerning the men seen running into the woods but the boy could not be induced to disclose the names of the men or tell where they were going. When an opportunity offered he slipped off the horse's back and made tracks for the house as fast as his little bare feet would carry him.

At the Peaslee home a number of large boys had assembled, Isaac's brother Joseph, Tom Curtis, John Sage, Smith Curtis, and Elliot Reed. The boys were standing near the house discussing the situation when two men were seen coming up through the fields from the direction of John Mayham's farm. They were the advance guard. Both had guns on their shoulders and came up directly to the place where the boys were standing.

Just at that moment Smith Peaslee left the house and started for the barn, carrying a basket of food for the men in the woods. The two men saw him and asked the boys who he was. Tom Curtis told them that he was a stranger. The men knew better and immediately gave chase. Smith saw them coming, wheeled around the corner of the barn within five hundred feet of them and started for the woods like a deer, still carrying the priceless basket. The men saw he could far outstrip them. Both raised their guns and fired with the result that he was hit in the back just above the hip. He did not slacken his speed however and was soon lost in the woods where he made his way to the camp and dropped exhausted.

The boys all saw the shooting as did also Mrs. Peaslee who was standing in the door of the house at the time. She recognized the men who did the shooting, one of whom belonged to a prominent and wealthy family residing in the south part of the town. She kept the knowledge to herself, however, and Smith Peaslee never knew who shot him. It was a cowardly act, with no warrant of law, but was in keeping with the general conduct of the posse while on that raid. Very likely Sheriff Brown and Under-sheriff Bouck did not sanction such acts, nor were all the men composing the posse guilty of such lawlessness. On the whole, however, the invading force was little better than a drunken mob, committing excesses that the Indians themselves had never dreamed of and sparing neither age, sex, nor condition, taking into custody boys who were guilty of no crime whatever and capturing men who had never worn a disguise nor violated a law.

CHAPTER XV

An Indian Shot

When Smith Peaslee rushed into camp with his basket of provision and fell in a dead faint it was thought at first that the cause was haste and excitement. In making an effort to revive him, blood was discovered upon his clothing and soon it became evident to all present that he had been shot. His clothing was quickly removed, the wound cleansed and the bleeding checked.

"This is an outrage," said John Mayham, the first to express an opinion.

"It is a damned outrage," said Dave Griggs, correcting the first speaker and at the same time reaching for his gun.

"Somebody will have to answer for this," he continued, grasping the weapon.

A dozen men got possession of their arms, angered beyond control. The wounded man now regained consciousness and was able to give some account of the shooting and also of the probable location of the posse.

"Don't waste any more time here boys," broke in Harry Wood, "come with me. They have commenced the shooting. We will give them all they want of it."

"And let's be mighty quick about it," put in Minard Veley, at the same time attending to the priming of his gun.

Sheldon Peaslee saw that the excited men meant to go in quest of the posse and give them battle on the spot. He saw also

Harry Wood

the full consequences of such a procedure for he knew that the men about him would shoot to kill. Once again his cool headedness was to save his neighbors.

"Hold boys," said he. "Murder will not help matters. If they come and attack us here, shoot to kill, but let them alone now."

"Yes," said Thomas Peaslee, in what was the most momentous crisis of his life. "The Almighty will avenge this deed. Stay your hand. Guard the camp well and if you are fired upon it will be time to defend yourselves. What say you John?"

"We will have the State troops here and the Devil to pay generally if we are not careful," replied John Mayham. "Let the posse do the shooting and we will keep out of the way. This thing cannot last. There is no law that will uphold a sheriff or his posse in such work as we have witnessed here today."

"Leave the work to me," said Smith Peaslee. "If ever I find who shot me I will shoot him like a dog." The hot Peaslee blood was up and if ever Smith Peaslee had known the man, he would have kept his word. As a matter of fact, Mrs. Peaslee kept the secret well and in after years the man who fired the gun was frequently a guest at the home of the man he shot. He, too, knew of the threat, and he, too, guarded the secret. Now, after more than sixty years, the name may stand in this history. In the last days of June, 1906, the writer spent a fortnight going over the territory which was the scene of these stirring events. The site of the old camp in the Hilton woods is very clearly marked. It is a circular space some thirty feet in circumference. The cattle seek out the clover there and keep the little space cropped short. There is a spring of clear cold water not far away. Following down towards the east, the old house where Sheldon Peaslee lived, and where the shooting occurred, is falling into decay, all excepting the cellar wall, which is as good today as when the stones were placed. Near by is the cluster of old orchard trees and, in the adjoining pasture, the clump of spice, a shrub found nowhere else in this part of the State. It has been growing here for nearly a century. In the woods, too, the vireo sings, a shy, sweet voiced songster, its clear peculiar note filling the whole forest. On to the east is the thirteen acre lot, now in grass, where the sixty horses belonging to the posse trampled down the standing rye. The foundation stones of John Mayham's log house still remain and the waters of the Schoharie are still seen away down through the mountains. Over on the Delaware road, the historian found an aged man, in his eightieth year, who went back in memory to the days of '45 and recounted the stirring incidents. This venerable man, Wm. Vroman, saw the anti-rent war on Blenheim Hill in its entirety. He was one of the prisoners captured and carried away to Gilboa and held there under the Inquisition. It was a pleasure to him to go over the old days and posterity will owe him its blessing therefor. His father, Thomas Vroman, "Long Tom," and "Santa Anna" of the Indian days, was one of the staunchest anti-renters in the community.

When, in the interview, this patriarch with white hair and beard was questioned about the shooting of Smith Peaslee, he gave the story vividly for he was present when it happened.

"And who did the shooting?" inquired the historian.

"Well sir," said he, with a keen twinkle in his eye, "it has generally been believed that Roman Gleason fired the gun."

Shortly after the shooting the main body of the posse came up with the advanced guard and were advised of what had happened. Under-sheriff Bouck protested against the unwarranted use of fire arms and a somewhat spirited discussion ensued in which mutiny was threatened, for a number of men who had been forced into the ranks at Blenheim and below declared that they would not be compelled to come up on Blenheim Hill and shoot men down in the fields.

"The sheriff gives no such orders," said Bouck.

"The damn rebels ought to be shot," put in an "up-renter" from Gilboa, and there were others from that locality who were like minded.

Sheriff Brown then ordered the posse to move forward to the residence of Thomas Peaslee and as that worthy could not be found they proceeded to the Brimstone church and encamped within its walls.

From the church predatory parties were sent out in various directions, spreading terror among the women and children. The posse kept clear of the woods where the Indian camp was located although they must have known something of its whereabouts. The fact was that even the bravest among them had no desire to come in close range of the Indian stronghold. The report that Smith Peaslee had been shot was soon made into a story that he had been killed and as the message gained distance it was changed to include his brother Sheldon and his father Thomas. The excitement became intense, not only among the people of Blenheim Hill and other localities but in the ranks of the posse as well, and a boy captive produced consternation in the Brimstone church by revealing there that he was a messenger sent to bring word from Dutch Hill that Red Jacket was on his way over at the head of a thousand armed Indians. Sheriff Brown did not credit the story but it was only by the show of authority that he could keep the posse from breaking cover and taking leg bail for Blenheim and Gilboa.

A runner had been sent to Dutch Hill however and a strong force was collecting there. Horns and signal fires thoroughly aroused the whole territory and every Indian was astir throughout Blenheim, Fulton, Jefferson, and Summit.

When Abe Spickerman got tidings of the raid and of the shooting he swore as only a Dutchman can. Those of the present generation, who remember the old gentleman and recall the impediment in speech which made it difficult for even his friends to understand him, will know how useless it would be to attempt to quote him in print. But what he lacked in clearness he more than made up in earnestness and if he could have had his way the whole Fulton tribe would have advanced upon Blenheim Hill at double quick and utterly annihilated the sheriff and his posse. Abe Spickerman was an anti-renter, heart and soul.

CHAPTER XVI

Boy Prisoners

D r. Cornell, the "old news carrier," as the up-renters called him, was far away in Columbia County when the posse reached the Hill on the 4th of August. A detachment visited his home, however. Two of his little children, John and Bettie, had raised a pole from one corner of the corn-house and from it floated a little flag that the children had made. This emblem of anti-rentism caught the eye of the commander of the posse and he ordered "six of his best men" to dismount and tear down the rebel ensign. This order was given with a strong oath and at that moment Mrs. Cornell appeared at the door.

"By all means send six of your best men. Two of my little children made the flag and put it up themselves. It will surely need six strong men to tear it down."

Bettie and John in the meantime had fled into the house and taken refuge on a bed in the recess. The older boys hid in the barn. A thorough search was made of the premises, including every room in the house. When they came to the bed one of the men said to Mrs. Cornell:

"Get those damn brats off of that bed. You have got them there to conceal the old man. We will find him between the ticks."

The children were roughly pulled from the bed and the coverings thrown upon the floor but no man was found. The boys in the barn were discovered and brought out in front of the house. Again Mrs. Cornell came to the door and addressed the men, "You have no right to touch those boys. Let them alone."

"We had just as soon shoot them as not," said the commander, "and we are going to make them prisoners."

"Come here Sime," said his mother, speaking to one of the boys.

"He can't come," said a member of the posse.

"I only want him to get his coat," said Mrs. Cornell, at which he was permitted to enter the house. The boy thought his mother intended to aid him to escape and he slipped away and entered a hallway at which two men sprang by Mrs. Cornell and grabbed the boy again, pulling him back into the room. As they did so one of them fell full length upon the floor for he was drunk.

"Call your men off and get them sober," said Mrs. Cornell to the commander, "before you give over some young boys into their charge. This whole proceeding is a disgrace. If my husband were here—"

"Your husband is here," broke in the commander, "and he is the man we are after."

"Why don't you search the place thoroughly then," said the good lady. "There is one building down yonder that you have missed," pointing at the same time towards a small structure about four feet square standing some six or eight rods from the house. Four or five men, not sober enough to comprehend where they were going, made a rush for the place and forced their way inside, only to return swearing for Mrs. Cornell had sent them on a fool's errand.

Convinced at last that Dr. Cornell could not be found, the posse prepared to move on and take the boys with them.

"Do not be afraid boys," said Mrs. Cornell as they moved away, "these men dare not hurt you."

The prisoners were conducted to the Brimstone church and placed under guard there.

Dr. Richtmyer Hubbell
Native of Blenheim Hill and present owner [1906] of about
fifteen hundred acres of Blenheim Hill anti-rent soil

In the meantime other detachments of the posse were oper-
ating at various places on the Hill. The men, of course, were all
in hiding, even the up-renters, for the officers treated all alike
now and visited every home in search of tenants, no matter what
their attitude had been on the question of rent. Mrs. B. P. Curtis had seen a number of horsemen pass through the fields near
her house and sent her young son Jacob to see if they had left the

bars down so that the cattle could get out of the pasture. The boy crept cautiously along the wall to a big cherry tree in the corner of a field of oats and wheat. There he came suddenly upon the posse. As he jumped over the fence they raised their guns and commanded him to stop, threatening to shoot him. He paid no attention to their orders but dashed away through the standing wheat, making for the woods. He ran so fast that he lost both shoes but kept up the pace until he reached the house where he found his brother Orrin and his sister Marie alone, their mother having gone to the neighbors. Very soon Elizabeth Elliot came down from the hill and said the posse was coming that way. The boys hid in the cellar behind some potato barrels. The posse entered the house and inquired for the inmates. Miss Elliot was a truthful old maid and told them that, besides the little girl and herself, there was no one else in the house excepting two small boys hiding in the cellar. The boys heard this and concluded to retreat to the barn where they climbed upon the mow and drove under the hay. The posse, not being able to find them, left the place, and the boys got down from the mow and ran through the lots in the direction of the Elliot farm. They encountered the posse again near the Maham place and hid behind the fence but a file of men with loaded guns and fixed bayonets came upon them and took them prisoners, carrying them to Elliot's barn.

Orrin could not be induced to talk at all and Jacob answered the questions put to them, which related to the identification of Indians. Finally one of the posse, a dark featured man with straight black hair, said, "I have been dressed as an Indian myself."

"You would not have to dress much," said the boy, "you look near enough like an Indian now to pass for one in our tribe."

"Not so saucy boy, or we will put you in jail," responded the man and the boy was scared into silence.

Abbie Elliot now came to the barn and gave the men a tongue-lashing, which was richly deserved. Finally, after being unable to get any information from the boys, they were released on account of their age, the youngest being only eight or nine and the other only a year or two older.

These boys might have imparted some interesting information, however, had they chosen to do so for they were acquainted with many of the secrets of the Indians. An older brother, Dorris, dressed as a squaw and given to all sorts of pranks, had carried the tar-bucket on more than one night raid and the father was one of the most trusted advisers at the council fires. An uncle, Josiah Curtis, father-in-law of Sheldon Peaslee, was likewise an Indian whose name struck terror to the heart of every member of the posse. He was a small man, weighing about 120 pounds, but could whip anything in the country. He had been known to turn a hand spring, kick a man with both feet full in the face and land upon his body as he fell. He could catch a man by the ankles and throw him flat upon his back. Two members of the posse brought him to bay that day. He had them both whipped in less than two minutes and then, starting on a run in the direction of a dozen more who were spectators some six or eight rods away, they, profiting by the experience of their companions, took flight to a man.

Jo Curtis could catch a chipmunk anywhere on a rail fence and was the wizard of all stone bees and logging camps. One time at Albany he whipped the bully of the city on the street in the sight of two policemen who afterward came to him and insisted upon paying his hotel bill as a consideration for the good services rendered.

CHAPTER XVII

"I Guess Not, by Hokey-Nettie"

For the first two or three days the members of the posse directed their efforts to the capture of Dr. Cornell, Thomas Peaslee, B. P. Curtis and Thomas Vroman but without success. They gathered in some twenty boys however, and kept them prisoners in the Brimstone church. Finally a number of men came and gave themselves up, chiefly to get inside the church and see that no harm came to the boys who were held there. A few "up-renters" had remained at home and kept at work, thinking they would not be molested, but these soon got word that the sheriff was no respecter of persons and that safety lay only in flight. Uncle Ben Kenyon took to the woods like an ordinary Indian when his arrest was attempted. A company of mounted men visited the home of Giles S. Champlin while he was at a spring some thirty rods away after two pails of water. His wife stepped to the door and gave a lusty blast on a horn as a danger signal and he left the pails at the spring and ran eastward, never stopping until he was safe on the Quarry mountain, a mile away. From his station in a tall hemlock he could see the bayonets glisten as the posse surrounded his house and searched the place. It was then that he experienced a change of heart, and as he often said afterwards, he felt like a fighting Indian while in the tree-top. The feeling grew on him, too, as he remained on the mountain several days living on blackberries, not daring to go home until he saw the signal

Giles S. Champlin

smoke which finally told him that there was no more danger. He was a good enough Indian after that and never again attempted to champion the cause of a landlord. In fact, long years after, it became known that both Giles Champlin and John Mayham "wore the calico" at the great Summit meeting and also upon other occasions away from home, though neither of them ever put on the disguise on Blenheim Hill.

By the middle of the week the posse had a number of prisoners under guard in the old church and preparations were made to take them to Gilboa. Mrs. John Warner, more brave perhaps than women in general, appeared at the church and demanded the release of her boys. No attention was paid to her but the good woman entered the church and told the boys to come with her. Then, defying the guard, she walked boldly out again and actually brought the boys home with her.

After several days in hiding, Jacob Shaver found his curiosity getting the better of him, and on the morning when the posse and prisoners were to start for Gilboa he crawled up along the wall south of the church in order that he might see what was happening. Slowly and cautiously he made his way until near the road and only a few rods from the church. Then, as he raised his head a little above the wall to get a good view of the proceedings, a member of the posse saw him and gave the alarm. A general shout followed at which Jake, either through fright or for some other reason, leaped upon the wall and stood in full view. The proceeding was so unexpected that for a moment the officers were bewildered. Just then Jake took off his hat and, swinging it high above his head, gave a most unearthly yell. The war-whoop aroused the sheriff to his duty and he commanded his men to take the rebel. Jake was so near the posse that he heard the order distinctly. Some two dozen or more mounted men started immediately in his direction, the foremost shouting to him to surrender.

"I guess not, by hokey-nettie," shouted the now thoroughly frightened Indian and, again swinging his hat and giving one more deafening yell, he sprang from the wall and bounded away through the meadow, the horsemen after him at full speed. Jake made directly for the tall swale grass and forest of cat-tails growing only a few rods away and reached the swamp ahead of the horses. Once among the bogs he was safe, for the horses sank to their knees, stumbled and fell, throwing their riders in every direction. In fact, the posse had started with such speed and so suddenly did they find themselves unhorsed that Jake easily made his escape while the men who were after him were a struggling mass trying to free themselves from the treacherous mire. Jake, however, never slackened his speed. On the contrary, once out of the cat-tails he ran all the harder down through the pines and over among the maples in Wm. Champlin's sap-bush. Nor

Col. John R. Sage

did this distance satisfy him, for he continued on over the burnt hill and approached his home from the south-east with as much precaution as a hunted fox. Arriving at last in the presence of his faithful wife, who met him with open arms, he exclaimed, "By hokey-nettie Lettie, they didn't get me, *surten* they didn't. My good legs saved me this time."

The posse made one capture that morning however. Coming back swearing from the swamp, someone called out, "There goes another damned rebel." A man was seen making through the fields at the top of his speed. The horsemen took after him, this time over dry ground. The Indian ran with all possible speed until he reached a brush fence when, ostrich-like, he thrust his head into the thick brush and lay perfectly still. The officers were upon him in an instant but the sight of him made them pause and convulsed them with laughter. After making him the subject of considerable banter one man finally prodded him with a bayonet at which he withdrew his head from the brush pile and said in most humble terms, "Gentlemen, I am as innocent as a lamb."

The posse carried him to the church, in spite of his innocence. Here he pleaded to be taken to his home that he might acquaint his wife of his plight. The request was granted and a squad conducted him to the house, only a short distance away.

"Mary Ann, let's repent," were the first words that greeted the frightened woman. And so far as was possible, this captured Indian did repent and readily told the sheriff all he knew about the Indians, which did not happen to be much, for while he had been a prominent speaker among them advocating tar and feathers when others used much milder language, they had never let him into the secrets of the tribe for they expected him to show the white feather. The posse held him however and carried him away to Gilboa.

Finally the boys were all released from the church and the older prisoners taken to Gilboa. This was towards the last of the week. In the meantime great events were happening in Delaware county and another posse from Delhi started for Blenheim Hill. But we must follow the prisoners. Among them were William Vroman, John, Philo, and Daniel Sage, Lyman Root, and Edward Wood. When they reached Gilboa they were confined in the tavern kept by Ira B. Rose. Oscar Howard and David Howard were stationed as guards over them. Then began a mock trial in the self-instituted court held by Gilbert R. Cumming, a young lawyer then practicing law in that village. The whole proceedings were illegal and aroused the greatest indignation. Some of the prisoners, among them John R. Sage, were at once released through the efforts of Luman Reed. The others, without counsel, were put through an examination. The questioning of William Vroman proved especially interesting. When at last the disgusted lawyer threatened to put him in jail unless he answered, he received this startling information:

You cannot get to Schoharie yourself. There are a thousand Indians in the mountains and along the rocks between Gilboa and Fulton and they will kill you as sure as the Almighty.

Towards the last of the week the anti-renters dispatched A. C. Morehouse to Cobleskill to obtain counsel, being anxious to secure either Thomas Smith or Jedediah Miller. However, before this narrative continues the account of Mr. Morehouse's night journey and the subsequent fate of the prisoners at Gilboa, it will be necessary to go back to that fatal Thursday at Andes and relate what was transpiring there, the day fixed for the sale on the farm of Moses Earle.

CHAPTER XVIII

Murder

It will be remembered that the adjourned sale on the premises of Moses Earle in Andes was to take place at one o'clock on Monday, Aug. 7, 1845. Sheriff More and Peter P. Wright arrived at the Earle farm about ten o'clock in the forenoon of that day where a number of men had already assembled. Mr. Wright accompanied the sheriff for the purpose of bidding on the property, that a sale might be made. They went at once to see Mr. Earle and proposed a settlement but he told the sheriff to go on and sell as he was determined to fight the case to the end. The sheriff reminded Mr. Earle that he had offered to settle but Mr. Earle said he had since changed his mind. It was evident that a large crowd was expected for sheep were being killed and dressed and other preparations were being made to provide entertainment for many people. This caused the sheriff to apprehend difficulty.

At eleven o'clock a company of six Indians, fully disguised and armed, were seen to cross the road from the north above the house and pass through the lot where the cattle that had been levied upon were, and enter the woods near the pasture where the sale was to take place.

"Command every spectator to assist in arresting those men," said Mr. Wright to the sheriff, and that officer did so. In the course of a quarter of an hour another small band of Indians passed into the woods. At noon a company of fifty Indians came out of the woods on the east side of the pasture and passed in single file to the woods on the south side where the others had congregated. At the same time fourteen more came off the side hill on the north side of the road and were passing in the direction of the others when Mr. Wright went up the road some forty rods east of the house and came within a few rods of them as they crossed the road and entered the pasture. Here they halted at the command of their chief and stood looking at Mr. Wright who was standing in the road. Some little conversation took place between the Indians and Mr. Wright when they finally passed on and he returned to the house.

Less than an hour later the Indians were observed coming out of the road on the south side of the pasture. They marched in single file and came up near the bars some fifteen or twenty rods east of the house on the south side of the road, where they formed in sections of four each and passed through the bars, forming in single line in the road, the lower end reaching opposite Mr. Earle's house. Mr. Wright was standing at the bars as the Indians passed. There were now fully one hundred of them, all armed, some with rifles, others with muskets, while many carried in addition small pistols, tomahawks, and bags of feathers. Mr. Wright started down the line when he met a chief who, raising his sword, commanded him to stand back.

"I will not stand back one inch for you or any of your tribe," said Mr. Wright, whereupon the chief placed his sword against Mr. Wright's breast and again ordered him back.

Placing his hand upon his pistol, Mr. Wright said, "Withdraw your sword or I will make a hole through you."

"Shooting is a game two can play," said the chief, dropping his sword and grasping his pistol.

"Lay hand on me and I will kill you. I am acting within the law and am here about my business. I do not fear you nor any of your tribe. You are all a pack of outlaws and cowards and you ought all to be in State prison. You all know that you are breaking the law," said Mr. Wright in a loud voice.

"Damn the law, we mean to break it," said the chief.

"I know who you are and will send you to prison," said Mr. Wright.

"You can't swear to me," replied the chief.

"Do you mean to bid on these cattle?" asked the chief.

"I came for that purpose."

"Then you will go home feet foremost in a wagon."

"I shall bid on this stock if I get a chance."

"And you know what will happen to you if you do."

Just at that time a pail of whiskey was brought out of Mr. Earle's house and carried along the line from which the Indians drank. Horns were blown and accessions were made to the Indian ranks. About half an hour later officers Steele and Edgerton came in sight, riding on horseback. It was two o'clock. The Indians marched forward against the stone wall on the north side of the road and about-faced. The sheriff announced that he would proceed with the sale and started for the pasture to drive up the stock. The chief then called for a dozen volunteers to accompany him to the lot in order to see that the sheriff did not sell the property down in the lot.

The sheriff, with some difficulty, drove the stock up near the bars but the Indians prevented their being taken into the road. The line of Indians by the wall then marched into the pasture and formed a hollow square around the bars, enclosing the cattle and the sheriff. Steele, Edgerton, and Wright were standing by the bars when Steele proposed to drive the cattle into the road. His right to do so was questioned by one of the anti-renters named Brisbane.

"We have a right to sell anywhere on the premises," said Steele, "and want the cattle in the road for the convenience of the bidders."

"The notice of sale defines the place of sale," said Brisbane, "and it is not in the highway."

Steele and Edgerton then rode down to the barn to examine a notice that was posted on the door. The Indians, supposing that these officers had started for home, ran into the road to head them off. Steele and Edgerton returned to the bars and the Indians went back into the field. Wright then went to the sheriff and said to him that unless the Indians would permit the property to be driven into the road he had best adjourn the sale. The sheriff replied that he thought he could get the cattle into the road all right. Brisbane and the sheriff continued to discuss the matter when Wright attempted to approach the sheriff. A platoon of Indians guarded the bars and forbid him to pass, and raising a gun and threatening to shoot him if he did so. Holding his cane in both hands, he placed it against the breast of the Indian who had threatened him and forced a passage into the lot, the Indians at the bars closing in behind him. Steele and Edgerton, appreciating his danger, rode into the lot about two lengths of their horses and Wright stood near the horses' heads. The file of Indians at the bars fell back, forming a semi-circle around the three men. Steele then commanded the Indians to give way, as he intended to aid More in driving out the stock. Steele now displayed great anger and expressed his determination of getting the cattle into the road at all hazards, at the same time drawing out his pistol. The chief then gave the command, "Shoot the horses, shoot the horses!"

Someone among the Indians called out, "Shoot him, damn him, shoot *him*."

The spectators at the bars moved away and thirty or forty rifles were pointed at the three men. Steele and Edgerton then, as officers of the law, commanded the peace, and Edgerton, in a loud voice, called upon every citizen present to assist in preserving the peace. A volley of rifles was then fired, Edgerton's horse was killed and Steele was wounded in the arm. Steele then fired into the crowd and his shot was answered by a second volley which came like a shower upon him, killing his horse, and he fell bleeding to the ground, three balls having pierced his body.

Sheriff More called out, "For God's sake men, desist. You have done enough."

Edgerton and Young ran and lifted Steele and asked him how badly he was hurt.

"Two balls have passed through me," said the dying man, "and my bowels are all shot to pieces." The two men carried him into Mr. Earle's home. He lived for five or six hours, enduring the most excruciating pain. While lying upon his bed in the agonies of death, Steele told Mr. Earle that if he had paid his rent the shooting would not have occurred. Earle replied that he would not pay it if it cost forty lives.

The Indians remained upon the ground but a very short time after the shooting and no further attempt was made at opening the sale. A messenger was dispatched for Mrs. Steele, who arrived just before the death of her husband which occurred early in the evening.

The death of Steele produced the greatest excitement and on the day following, Friday, couriers were dispatched to Albany to confer with the Governor. A posse was hurried into Roxbury to arrest Warren P. Scudder who had acted as chief at the sale on the day that Steele was shot. Men came pouring into Delhi to tender their services in searching for those who had been present in disguise at the time of the murder and many companies were sent out in various directions, one of which proceeded to Blenheim Hill. As the week drew to a close the prisoners were still being held at Gilboa, the Backbone Indians were arranging an important meeting, A. C. Morehouse was making his way to Cobleskill after counsel, and the wildest stories were in circulation.

CHAPTER XIX

End of the War

*W*hen the posse finally departed from Blenheim Hill with their prisoners, as related in a previous chapter, the men in hiding appeared again and counseled together. The interior of the Brimstone church was a perfect wreck, rendered so by members of the posse who had encamped therein. The anti-rent pole had been cut down by order of Jake Allen, the commander from Gilboa. Scarcely a farm in the community had escaped the destructive work of the officers of the law. It was decided to get together at the old church on Saturday and one of the first things to be done would be the raising of another anti-rent pole. Two fine walnuts were secured and spliced, James Van Dusen making the iron bands which held them together.

Early Saturday forenoon several hundred men assembled, many in disguise, with Thomas Vroman as Santa Anna acting as chief. Very soon the tall hickory pole stood upright and firmly fixed in the earth and another and larger flag waved from the top, still proclaiming the sentiments of the people: DOWN WITH THE RENT. Thomas Peaslee and John Mayham addressed the multitude, dwelling on the outrages committed by the posse and suggesting plans to secure the release of their neighbors held in custody at Gilboa. Probably many of the men present expected that the Indians were to march that day to Gilboa and release the prisoners and most of them were anxious to do so. As yet no

Shew Hollow Church

word had been received from Andes and nothing was known about the results of the attempted sale on Thursday, the shooting of Steele, or his death on Thursday night. It was known however that A. C. Morehouse had started the night before for Cobleskill after counsel, but it was feared that even if he succeeded in getting a lawyer the attorney would be arrested as David Smith had been when he volunteered to defend the prisoners. The sentiment of the meeting strongly favored going to Gilboa, but just before a final vote was taken a horseman was seen galloping eastward on the Delaware road. His message was quickly delivered. It told of the shooting and death of Steele, of the search being made for Scudder, and of the probable coming, that day, of a posse from Delhi. This news created the greatest excitement. The idea of going to Gilboa was at once abandoned and a hurried agreement was reached to hold no further meetings, each anti-renter to act alone thereafter. The company very

quickly dispersed, and in the course of the day some of the released prisoners arrived home from Gilboa, among them Lyman
Root. It was fortunate that the shoemaker reached home that
day for he had important work to do that night.

Warren P. Scudder, after the shooting of Steele, returned to
his home in Roxbury, and the next day worked at plowing as
though nothing had happened. Towards night a messenger appeared and warned him to flee, telling him that the officers
knew that he had acted as chief at the sale on the previous day.
He immediately left his work and consulted with his father, who
advised him to make his way if possible to Blenheim Hill where
he would find friends. His escape that night was prevented by
the speedy appearance of officers from Delhi. A hiding place
had already been provided on the Scudder farm and here the
man remained secluded for a day while the officers made a
thorough search of the place, remaining until Saturday morning. When evening came, Scudder started alone for Blenheim
Hill and made his way thither with no difficulty, reaching
Lyman Root's before midnight. The shoemaker was aroused,
took in the fugitive and tapped his boots by candle light, after
which he conducted Scudder to the home of Thomas Vroman,
who hid him away safely in his barn. By this time the escape of
Scudder was causing the authorities of Delaware county considerable uneasiness and bands of men were out searching the
country in every direction.

When the news of the shooting of Steele reached Gilboa
the up-renters were furious and even threatened to hang the
prisoners from Blenheim Hill. The posse made preparations to
return to the Backbone and arrest the remainder of the male in-
habitants, provided they could be captured. The preacher,
Moses Pendal, was particularly wrought up in the matter and
spent Sunday collecting guns and loading them for the posse to
carry on their second raid after Blenheim Hill Indians. This
dominie had held revival meetings in the Brimstone church

and had been fed and supported by the very men whose blood he now proposed to spill. This was more than Bill Vroman could stand and he proceeded to speak his mind freely to the minister.

"You infernal blackleg," said the irate prisoner, "stand here and load guns to shoot the very men who have put food into your mouth and clothes upon your back. Let the report of what you are doing once get back to Blenheim Hill and the men there will capture you and hang you from the high box pulpit in the old Brimstone church from which you have so often preached to them about the hell you will inhabit."

Keeping the prisoners quiet was no easy matter, for those held were all men disposed to make things lively. The house was crowded, the posse making it their headquarters as well as a prison, and by Sunday a goodly number of guests were ill with a common August ailment which poor whiskey did not alleviate. But that day Dr. Cornell came riding into Gilboa on his good cream nag, returning from Columbia county. The sheriff ordered his arrest because he was one of the chief characters among the Blenheim Hill Indians whose capture had been greatly desired. Just now, however, the sheriff was anxious to secure his professional services and he was requested to prescribe for the sick men without delay. The science of medicine in 1845 differed somewhat from that of the present day though physicians still sometimes believe in a thorough cleansing of the system. That was Dr. Cornell's strong point. We are bound to believe that the Doctor acted strictly within the lines of his usual practice in those cases and with uniformly good results. Every member of the posse who took his medicine, and some fifty men did so, lived the strenuous life for a day or two, but with ultimate good results, for all soon recovered.

Lon Morehouse made his way on horseback Friday night, inquiring the directions with great caution, getting off the road more than once, and hearing all sorts of stories then afloat. He finally reached Cobleskill and secured a lawyer, making his journey homeward on Monday, through Jefferson, arriving at Blenheim that night.

On Monday, August 11, the Delhi posse, three hundred strong, under the command of officer Boughton, came from Roxbury through Moresville, now Grand Gorge, up to Blenheim Ridge and from there to Blenheim Hill. They halted on the Ridge to capture Amos Loper, a prominent Indian, but he got away from them. Perry Lane, now in his eightieth year, recalls the chase. He was raking oats in a field through which Loper ran at high speed with several members of the posse in full pursuit. He escaped to the woods and the posse went on to Blenheim Hill without him.

The coming of this large force to the Backbone frightened the people greatly but the officers and men conducted themselves like gentlemen. No outrages were committed though the search for Scudder was continued for several days. The Gilboa posse returned early in the week, bearing the guns that the dominie had loaded, but they did not use them. A number more prisoners were taken, some to be carried to Gilboa, others to Schoharie, and a few to Delhi. The men from Delhi and from Gilboa also, in visiting the farmhouses, would frequently find the places entirely deserted, even by the women and children. Sometimes meals would be ready on the table but no one in sight. In such cases the men usually helped themselves, even visiting cellars and cupboards in search of eatables. They also seized hay and grain from the barns for their horses, but there was no more wanton destruction of property as there had been during the previous week.

Thomas Smith, then one of the leading lawyers of Cobleskill, reached Gilboa early in the week and took up the defense of the prisoners. He dissolved the illegal, self-constituted court, set the prisoners free, and threatened the military guards with State prison. He also notified the invading force from Delaware county that they had exceeded their authority, and the Delaware posse retreated. The sheriff of Schoharie county dismissed his men, and the war on Blenheim Hill was over, though Scudder was all the time concealed in Thomas Vroman's barn. His escape from there and subsequent events in the Steele tragedy will be made the subject of the next chapter.

CHAPTER XX

Reaction

arren P. Scudder lay concealed in Thomas Vroman's barn on Blenheim Hill for several days while the officers of Delaware and other counties were searching everywhere for him. Finally he was taken to the deserted camp in the Hilton woods and kept there about a fortnight, the Peaslees providing him with food. About the 1st of September he was conducted one night to the home of Henry Cleveland on Dutch Hill. Here he had an interview with Cornelius Maham, then a resident of that community, who advised him not to tarry in that locality. The next night he was taken to the home of Jay Tompkins on Rossman Hill and from there made his way to Canada. After an absence of several years, Scudder returned to Delaware county where he was at once arrested but was never brought to trial.

On August 27, 1845, Governor Silas Wright issued a proclamation declaring Delaware county in a state of insurrection. Adjutant General Farrington of Oswego proceeded to Delhi and took command of two companies of volunteers, forming them into a battalion of light infantry. Their officers were: captain, Benjamin T. Cook, Franklin; lieutenant, William Buckingham, Harpersfield; ensign, Angus McDonald, Jr., Stamford. Of the second company: captain, John R. Baldwin, Stamford; lieutenant, Thomas E. Marvine, Walton; ensign, Palmer L. Burrows, Tompkins.

Officers and soldiers now scoured the country arresting suspects and in the course of a few weeks the Delhi jail was full of anti-renters awaiting trial. Finally the number became so large that two log prison pens were hastily constructed and filled with men.

On September 8, the Sessions Court of Delaware county convened and in the course of the next two weeks indictments were found against two hundred and forty-two persons. The Circuit Court met on September 22, Judge Parker presiding. The trials were long and would be tedious in recital. Two of the prisoners, John Van Steenburgh and Edward O'Conner, were convicted of murder, four were sentenced to State prison for life, and about a dozen more for a term of years. There was no evidence to show that either Van Steenburgh or O'Conner were actually guilty of the killing of Steele. No one knew and no one could know who fired the shots that caused his death. The convictions were in a measure political ones, though the trials were fair and the verdicts within the law. Judge Parker, in passing sentence upon the prisoners, stated that they were among the two hundred disguised and armed men present when Steele was shot and that they were thus clearly guilty of murder under the law, even if they did not fire. Both men were accordingly sentenced to be hung on November 29, 1845. Governor Wright commuted the sentences of the two condemned men to imprisonment for life and later Governor John Young pardoned them, together with all other anti-renters under sentence.

Soon after the discharge of the Blenheim Hill prisoners held at Gilboa, as related in the last chapter, the landlords and their agents proposed a settlement whereby those tenants who desired were permitted to buy the soil at a nominal price per acre and most of the farms on the Backbone were speedily released from feudal tenure. A few farms, however, continued under the old arrangement and even to this day there is here and there a small tract of lease land.

Wood Homestead

To return to the exciting days of August. The funeral of
Steele was attended by two thousand people, and meetings were
held simultaneously at various places in Delaware and adjoining
counties at which speeches were made and resolutions passed
condemning the lawlessness of the Indians and deprecating all
forms of resistance to the laws. At the Stamford meeting A. M.
Babcock presided. Isaac D. Cornwall, Charles Griffin, Calvin
C. Covil, Joshua Draper, Hiram Fredenburgh, and Adam Grant
were appointed to a committee to draft resolutions to express
their indignation and extend sympathy. On December 22 the
Governor revoked his insurrection proclamation and the militia
was discharged from active service. Subsequently, at the village
of Delhi, a monument was erected to Steele as a faithful officer
who had fallen while in the fulfillment of his duty.

By the end of 1845 a reaction set in and that part of the anti-
rent contest which had been characterized by violent opposition

Clark Homestead

to law and by general disorder was at an end. It still remained a living question, however, in the courts, in the legislature, in the constitutional convention, and in the State at large.

In the heated contest for the governorship in 1846, John Young, the Whig candidate, is said to have pledged himself to pardon all the anti-renters who were in prison. The anti-renters supported him loyally and he was elected, though the remaining candidates on the Democratic ticket were elected. On January 27, 1847, in less than one month after his inauguration, Governor Young issued a proclamation stating that he held petitions from more than 11,000 persons asking the pardon of the men convicted of offences growing out of the so-called anti-rent excitement. He reviewed the whole series of occurrences and stated his belief that the spirit of lawlessness had entirely passed away, and that, as the offences were political in their nature, the ends of the law had been fully subserved by the imprisonment of its subjects for a period which had already extended to two years. He then proceeded to declare pardon to the eighteen still remaining in State prisons, and restored the greater number of them to citizenship.

In the legislative session of 1845 the most vigorously contested measure was the proposal to hold a State convention in the following year to form a new constitution. The anti-renters of course favored this action, as they had more to hope from a fundamental change in the laws with regard to the tenure of land than from mere legislative enactments. To this end, petitions were laid before the legislature bearing 25,000 signatures, and representing fifteen counties. John Mayham of Blenheim Hill was one of the most active men in this matter, taking up his residence in Albany for a time and appearing before the legislative committees again and again. It was largely through his influence, and by the help of the anti-rent members of the legislature, that the constitutional convention bill was passed, and when the convention met in 1846 the general feeling was in favor of some modification of the law in the direction of the views of the anti-renters.

In his annual message of January, 1846, Governor Young reviewed the history of the anti-rent difficulties and recommended the passage of several measures. These were: first, that distress for rent, in the case of leases made in the future, should be abolished; secondly, that the landlord should be taxed on that part of his income derived from rent; and thirdly, that the duration of the time of all leases to be made in the future should be restricted to a small number of years. These recommendations, which had for the most part appeared before previous legislatures but reported adversely, were now referred to committees of the two houses, that of the assembly being under the able chairmanship of Samuel J. Tilden of Columbia county. To the committees were also referred the various petitions of the tenants. Hearings were given to counsel of the proprietors of Rensselaer

Manor and to representatives of the tenants from Schoharie, Delaware, Albany, Schenectady, Montgomery, and Greene. The committees also examined a large number of deeds, leases, and other sources of information. The report of the Assembly Committee was made March 28, 1846 and, from its thorough and broad-minded character, is worthy of detailed consideration. It foreshadowed the open and honest statesmanship of Samuel J. Tilden, destined to become one of the foremost public men in his State and in the Nation.

CHAPTER XXI

Articles of Agreement

*I*n the report of the Assembly committee, made March 28, 1846, strong mention was made of the unfavorable influences of leasehold tenures and restraints upon alienation. The abolition of distress for rent and the limitation of the period of the leases to be made in the future were recommended.

When the constitutional convention of 1846 assembled the anti-rent element was strong enough to secure the following:

The people of this State, in their right of sovereignty, are deemed to possess the original and ultimate property in and to all lands within the jurisdiction of the State, and all lands the title to which shall fail from a defect of heirs, shall revert or escheat to the people.

All feudal tenures of every description, with all their incidents, are declared to be abolished, saving, however, all rents and services certain which at any time heretofore have been lawfully created or reserved.

All lands within this State are declared to be allodial, so that, subject only to the liability to escheat, the entire and absolute property is vested in the owners, according to the nature of their respective estates.

No grant or lease of agricultural land for a longer period than twelve years, hereafter made, in which shall be reserved any rent or service of any kind, shall be void.

All fines, quarter sales, or other like restraints upon alienation, reserved in any grant of land hereafter to be
made, shall be void.

During and subsequent to the anti-rent agitation, a great
proportion of the lands affected became the absolute property of
their occupants through purchase. In this connection the following document is of two-fold interest. It outlines the probable
terms of settlement between John A. King and the tenants of
Blenheim and it also gives the names of many of the men who
were active in the anti-rent times.

We the Undersigned, Lessees of John A. King, Esq., do
hereby mutually agree each with the other and each for
himself as follows, viz:

First, That we will offer to the said John A. King the
sum of Twenty-five thousand dollars in full consideration
for a conveyance in Warrantee of all his right, title and
interest in the lands known as the Blenheim and Baffington Patents containing Fifteen thousand four hundred and
ninety acres or at the same rate be the same more or less.

Second, that we will individually pay our proportions of
the said sum of Twenty-five thousand dollars in the manner following: Those lessees in occupancy of land at a Rent
charge of Twenty cents per acre to pay at the rate of one
dollar eighty-seven and a half cents per acre. Those in occupancy of land at a rent charge of Fifteen cents per acre to
pay at the rate of one dollar and fifty-five cents per acre.
And those in occupancy of land at a rent charge of Twelve
and a half cents per acre to pay at the rate of one dollar and
fifty cents per acre.

Third, We do further agree to select a Committee to act
as our duly authorized agents to enter into a Contract with
the said King for the sale and purchase of his said lands on

the terms above mentioned it being hereby expressly stipulated and agreed that in case the said King accepts our proposition as above stated he shall upon payment of the sums due from us individually under such contract execute to each of us a Warrantee Deed of such lands as we may purchase at the rate above mentioned.

And we do further agree that every lessee who shall pay to the said King, his due proportion of the said purchase money as above mentioned, on or before the 15th day of November, A.D., 1847, shall be exonerated from all liabilities or charges arising under this agreement upon payment of a sum of money to the said committee, equal to an assessment of Five per cent upon the purchase money paid by each lessee. And in case any lessee shall pay a sum less than his due proportion, for the purpose of extending his time of payment, he shall pay five per cent to the said committee on the amount so paid and ten per cent upon the amount remaining unpaid, provided that no such term of payment shall extend over three years from the said 15th November.

And it is hereby understood and agreed that this article of agreement shall be of no effect unless subscribed by a majority of all the tenants of the said Blenheim and Baffington Patents.

Dated January 6, 1847.

Henry Simons	John Mayham
Soloman Franklin	R. W. Ruliffson
Reuben Franklin	S. C. Cole
George Franklin	Thomas S. Peaslee
Wm. B. Champlin	J. R. Sage
Henry N. Maynard	G. S. Champlin
Christopher Kniskern	Daniel Sage 2d
Joshua Tompkins	John B. Vroman

William P. Champlin
George H. Champlin
Hiram Huftaling
Harmon Ruliffson Jr.
Milo Wood
Daniel Sage
Edward Wood
Caleb Hastings
Luther Hastings
Thomas Vroman
David Reed
H. Goodenough
John Beach
Peter Brady
Owen Smith
John M. Haines
John Franklin
Alanson Topping
J. White
Seth Brown
Clark Franklin
Zeke Brockway
——Ames
Jesse M. Cornell
Peter I. Harder
Jacob H. Miller
Abram H. Foot
Benjamin Vandusen
Abraham Pindar
Henry H. Myers
Elam Gallup
Patrick Gallacher
William H. Lyon

Charles Maham
Christopher Decker
Thomas Peaslee
George W. Martin
J. W. Atchinson
Let Perry
Peleg Simmons
Wm. Mayham
David Smith
William Vroman
William Jump
William Jump Jr
John Perry
Stephen Perry
William Perry
Orrin Clark
David Baley
Robert Baley
Cornelius Baley
Thomas Lines
John Cornell
Lewis Shelmandine
Peter I. Decker
Selar Decker
David J. Proper
David Proper
Henry Cleveland
Henry Gardner
Henry Ploss
Winthrop Dyer
B. P. Curtis
David Craton
Casper Martin

Philo Johnson
Stephen G. Champlin
John Hendrick
Mathias Benjamin
Samuel L. Eggleston

Lemuel D. Pierce
Benjamin Frazee
Jacob R. Hubbell
Jonathan Winnie

CHAPTER XXII

The Letter of a Landlord

The following letter, though of a date prior to that of the agreement given in the last chapter, and, in fact, earlier by a year than the actual conflict on Blenheim Hill, will be read with greater interest in the light of the history already given. It was issued in the form of a circular and distributed generally among the tenants on the Blenheim patent.

JAMAICA, L. I., July, 1844.

Sir:—Early in April last, I was informed of your fixed purpose to refuse and resist the payment of Rent to me; and soon afterwards of your having met in large numbers, in different parts of the Patent of Blenheim, for the purpose for forming yourselves into an Anti-Rent Society; and as the most effective mode of carrying out your deliberate intentions in this respect, that you had proceeded to pass resolutions, denying the validity of my title; refusing to pay any more Rent; raising money to defray all expenses and costs, to which, as a consequence of such determination you might be subjected; and requiring also, that a certain number of your members should disguise themselves as Indians, who, by threats of personal violence, should prevent my agent, or the Officers of the Law, from collecting the Rent, respectively due from you. Whatever grievance, if any, others may have—whatever grounds of complaint, well or ill-founded, may exist as to the tenure, by which others hold Lease-land—certain I am, you, at least, have none. Since this property came into my possession on which you live, and from whose soil is drawn, not only your own support, but the small Rent stipulated to be paid by you for the use and occupation of the same, you have been treated with a liberality and fairness, which should rather have strengthened the relations which exist between us, than have furnished the ground for the denial of my Title, and the state of feeling and excitement, and the refusal to pay, which now so extensively prevails among you. I neither know, nor do I care to know, who, and what they are, that have thus caused you to swerve from your free and self-incurred obligations to pay Rent for the Lands you have leased of me—Lands, which have been in my possession, and in the possession of those from whom I derive my Title, since the year 1788—Lands, which when they became mine, about the year 1830, for a full and valuable consideration, were greatly in arrears for Rent, were, in many instances, subject to a Wheat Rent, and that payable in Albany, at a great distance from the residence of you all. I came among you, as soon as these Lands were mine; I saw you, heard your story, settled with each of you upon terms and conditions, which you admitted were liberal and satisfactory. From time to time for many years, I have been among you; and never, without those feelings of pride and confidence, which was the result of the relations which existed between us. My great aim and desire were, to render you contented and happy, and I thought I had done so. Nor was this all; as churches were established among you, I gave to each denomination annually a contribution towards its support. And when you complained, that it was hard to carry the Wheat to Albany, in payment of your Rent, and that it could no longer be raised in Blenheim; I agreed to commute that payment in kind at Albany, for a Money Rent payable in Blenheim; and also to receive a certain sum in Cash per acre, as a commutation for the Wheat Rent; and forever after fifteen cents an acre in lieu of it. I offered, also, when you were all agreed to purchase the right, of soil, to sell to you at fair prices — thus removing all ground of objection to the payment of Rent under a durable Lease. In short, in all ways, and upon every occasion when we have met together, and through my Agent, who has lived among you for many years, and has always possessed your and my entire confidence, I have ever made it my duty to consult, so far as I could, the welfare, convenience, and ability of you all. You may judge then of the extreme surprise and regret, with which I received the intelligence of your determination to withhold the payments of your Rents, and of your combination to resist the collection of the same at all hazards. The first great principle of the moral law is, to do as you would be done by. Now, supposed the case reversed, and you the owner of the land, and I, by voluntary agreement, the Lessee of the same, bound to pay rent for its use and occupation; your means of supporting your family, and assisting your children, dependent upon, and derived from this property, lawfully yours, — what would you think, or how would you act, if seduced from my duty and my engagements, by the counsel of evil friends and advisers, I should first deny your Title, and then, as a natural consequence, refuse to pay Rent to you — your honest due — your lawful demand — what would be your course, under such circumstances, for the protection of your property, for the collection of your Rents? If I had dealt harshly with you; if I had exacted the last farthing; if I had shown, by my conduct and actions, that there was nothing in common between us — there might, perhaps, have been some reason

for your listening to the advice of evil counsellors, to the
influence and example of wrong-doers on other Patents.
Such a state of things you know, and I know, has never existed between us. Hence then, I repeat, you may judge of
my surprise and regret, on hearing of the proceedings in
which you have been engaged—and I now, after having
left you full time for reflection, and a safe and quiet return
to your obligations, make this appeal to you as men, as citizens bound by every legal and moral tie, to fulfil your
agreements—to cast off the evil counsellors, the interested
leaders, who have drawn you from the quiet path of duty,
and of voluntary contract, to enter upon that of contention, violence, and ultimate defeat and submission,—
choose you, then, while it is yet time, between him, who
has ever so far proved himself your friend, and those, who,
in an evil moment, and for interested and selfish purposes,
have wrought upon your feelings by false statements, to
do, what you have already done, and still propose to ac-
complish. I desire you to reflect upon what I have stated—
to be assured that there is no ground, not the slightest, for
the charge that my Title is defective—and which, you at
least, are prevented from questioning. I have foreborne,
and may yet for a while forbear, to enforce the collection of
my Rents by Law, and if need be, by the power of the
County. Yet, you must remember, that forbearance has its
limits; and that if you persist in your refusal to fulfil your
obligations, I shall be compelled to appeal to the Law, for
the vindication of my rights, and the enjoyment of my
property. I must defend and protect my interest in Blenheim, purchased for a large sum of money. Your denial of
my title, and refusal to pay rent, leave me no other
course,—and when that appeal is once made, the Law, and
it alone, must be the umpire between us. The decision of
this question rests with you—should it still continue to be

adverse to my rights, I shall as surely and as firmly rely upon a jury of my countrymen, as I have heretofore reposed confidence upon your good will and fidelity to your engagements. If you wish to see me, I am ready to come among you, whenever you shall inform my Agent, that you are prepared to receive me. In the mean time, ponder well, and reflect calmly upon the state of things which now exists between us—which cannot last—tread back your steps—comply with your contracts—be just to me, be just to yourselves.

Yours, &c.,

JOHN A. KING.

CHAPTER XXIII

Memories Differ

There are many little incidents connected with the anti-rent war that have come to light in the course of the preparation of this history but too late to be incorporated in proper chronological order. They have a part in the story and will be read with interest. It should also be stated that men who have been interviewed do not remember events alike nor do printed authorities agree.

Isaac Peaslee of Georgetown, California is positive that the raid on Blenheim Hill was made on Monday, August 4, 1845. It is certain that Steele was shot on Thursday, August 7. Several men say the raid was not made until after Steele was shot, among them Henry De Money, now 81 years old, who was a member of the Delhi posse. Perry Lane, in his eightieth year, says Amos Loper was not captured by the posse but escaped by fast running. George Monfort, nearly as old, is positive that Amos Loper was surprised and taken prisoner while at work in his shop. The general opinion is that Brown and Bouck were carried to Baldwin's mill on the West Kill. Mary Rockerfeller, 84 years old, says they were taken up the North Road and made to burn their papers in a field back of David Reed's.

The story of the capture of Brown and Bouck at Fink's tavern is told in many ways. There is no agreement as to who threw Bouck over the bar, some claiming that it was a young man named Sage, barely 20 years of age. William Vroman, who was not interviewed until after that chapter appeared in print, says the story as told is correct in every particular.

Rev. A. C. Morehouse, in his autobiography, says Scudder reached Lyman Root's on Blenheim Hill on the evening of the day following the shooting of Steele and infers that he went from there immediately to Dutch Hill, and from there to Rossman Hill where Jay Tompkins carried him to Westerlo, Albany county. There friends kept him secreted for months in a cave. This is very clearly a mistake. Scudder remained on Blenheim Hill for several weeks after the shooting according to the testimony of a number of men still living who saw him there and knew of his being cared for by Thomas Vroman and the Peaslees.

Morehouse is very evidently mixed in his story of the raid also. He says that Brown and Bouck were captured in July, 1845, and that a posse was organized at Schoharie right after that to arrest those who had participated in the violent treatment of the sheriffs. This might easily bring the raid on August 4, 1845, but the most positive testimony places the capture of Brown and Bouck in the winter time. Judge Stephen L. Mayham says it occurred in the spring of 1844, and that the two men were carried to Baldwin's mill in a sleigh. He is probably the only living witness to the event. He was a schoolboy at the time, boarding at Fink's tavern.

Morehouse must be right in his account of his journey to Cobleskill after counsel but he seems to be wrong in stating that the prisoners held at Gilboa were released on Friday upon parole to report on the following Monday. William Vroman, 80 years old and of sound mind and memory, who was one of the prisoners, is positive that they were not released. Again, the Morehouse account states that the Western tribe (Blenheim Hill) of Indians held a council of war on the day before he took his journey to Cobleskill and decided, after heated discussion, to make no more opposition to the landlords. The day of this meeting seems to be Friday, which must have been August 8. This would be very likely, provided the news of the shooting of Steele reached Blenheim Hill on that day, the day following his death. But it is quite evident that no word was received there until Saturday morning and it is also probable that Amos Loper conducted Scudder from the Ridge to Lyman Root's house on Saturday night. It must be, also, that Morehouse is mistaken when he says Jay Tompkins was absent from home when he called there on his way to Cobleskill, having gone to conduct Scudder to Westerlo. William Vroman is positive that there was a pole-raising near the Brimstone church on Saturday, August 9, and that news of the Steele tragedy came from the Head-of-the-river that forenoon.

Morehouse again states that, having lost his way and gone eight miles beyond Cobleskill, while eating breakfast at the hotel he found the greatest excitement, hearing that the Schoharie and Delhi posse had surprised a company of Indians on Blenheim Hill, shot a Methodist local preacher, and many more stories that he knew to be false. This was very likely on Sunday, August 10. The shooting must have been that of Smith Peaslee but that was certainly done by the Gilboa posse and before the shooting of Steele or the coming of the posse from Delhi.

Morehouse returned from Cobleskill on Monday by the way of Jefferson, he being a captain of the militia and compelled to appear at general training at that village on that day, but he says the officers were so few at Jefferson, on account of the great excitement, that those present were all relieved and dismissed. On his way to North Blenheim he must have gone down the North Road. He says he discovered two hundred citizens in a field near the road, three miles from his home, very likely near the Hilton place. They recognized him and shouted to him that Smith, the Cobleskill lawyer, had come. The purpose of this meeting of anti-renters is not clear and Morehouse says nothing more about it. Both the Schoharie and Delhi posse were searching the country at that time. These two hundred men must have known

Hon. Steppen L. Mayham
Judge of the Supreme Court
Born and reared on Blenheim Hill

of Steele's death and it was extremely dangerous for a company of tenants to be assembled.

Morehouse says of the action of Thomas Smith, the Cobleskill lawyer who went to Gilboa to effect the release of the Blenheim Hill prisoners:

His energetic manner of presenting the many mistakes of the authorities in arresting and confining those who were doing nothing at most but fleeing from the excited posse, who, in their new and supposed authority, had exercised what might be properly termed mob law, so impressed them that a compromise was effected, the prisoners all released, and a peaceful state of things comparatively reigned in Schoharie county.

Judge Mayham writes:

On the arrival of Mr. Smith, he at once broke up the illegal self constituted tribunal assuming to try these prisoners without authority of law. He also dissolved the military guards by giving them notice that unless they immediately released all prisoners held in custody by them, that they and their officers, sheriffs, constables, etc., would be prosecuted for false imprisonment. The invaders from Delaware county at once beat a hasty retreat and the posse from Schoharie followed their example and all of the prisoners found themselves at liberty to return to their homes.

The Delhi posse took David Reed prisoner when he was sick in bed. They thought he was feigning illness. He was placed upon a horse and started for Delhi. When they reached Dr. Hilton's residence the Doctor came out and ordered the officers to release the prisoner. He then took the sick man into his own house and cared for him until he recovered. This incident, related by a granddaughter of David Reed, would indicate that the Delaware posse took their prisoners to Delhi, a very likely proceeding, although most other authorities agree in saying that all prisoners taken on Blenheim Hill were carried to Gilboa.

In Chapter VII it is stated, on good authority, that John McEntyre of Gilboa was an Indian chief called Tecumseh. William Vroman declares this is positively an error, that McEntyre was an out and out up-renter and generally hated by the Indians. It is more than sixty years since the stirring days of the anti-rent war, and there is little wonder that all memories do not agree.

CHAPTER XXIV

After Sixty Years

The story of the anti-rent war has been told. The next chapter, dealing with the old manor-house in Blenheim, will complete the history. There yet remain a few reminiscences and these are given here. The testimony of eye witnesses is the best evidence. Few men and women remain who participated in the conflict and anything they say should be recorded.

Martin Van Buren Hager of North Blenheim, seventy-eight years old, remembers the capture of Brown and Bouck well. He says Bouck floored several strong men before he was overpowered. He also says that the two sheriffs were made to walk to Baldwin's mill in their stocking feet. During the night when the posse was at Fink's tavern, word came that the woods were full of Indians. The excited men rushed from the inn in their night clothes and began to shoot promiscuously in the darkness. Mr. Hager remembers Jay Tompkins well. He was an athlete. He could put one hand on the top rail of a high fence and clear it at a bound. He would often stand on one foot in the barroom of the old tavern, kick the ceiling and come back on the same foot.

George H. Ferguson of Richmondville says:

> The Summit Indians belonged to Red Jacket's tribe. After the shooting of Steele I had several suits and disguises

which I hid in the side hill on premises owned by J. B. Wharton. So far as I know there are there yet. Scudder was kept for a long time by Jay Tompkins about two miles from Sapbush Hollow. Jeremiah Colliton's wife, who lived with her husband on a farm in Summit, was an up-renter. She persisted in blowing her horn to call the help to meals. One noontime she blew the horn as usual and the men not responding, she went out behind the woods to blow the horn again. In her absence a dozen Indians made a raid upon her house, ate the good dinner she had prepared, and carried away all the eatables from the cellar and pantry.

Mrs. N. K. Hoagland of Schenevus writes:

I am a woman now seventy years of age and can very vividly remember the time of the anti-rent war. I was then at my father's home, John J. Warner on Blenheim Hill, a young girl in my early "teens." How distinctly I can remember the day and the scene when a large number of these up-rent men called the posse came to my father's house to further their cause, and the course mother took with them. She talked to them kindly and told them what the war was for and how unjust the rent was. She explained how they could not pay the rent demanded and support their family. She told them they were willing to pay a reasonable amount but the rent they demanded was too much and they had no right to exact such an exorbitant sum. She also told them she did believe they could show good title to the land from which they were collecting rent. Father was a prisoner in the Brimstone church on this day, which will explain why mother did the talking. It seems they did not know what they were making war over. One of the men said to mother: "Is that what we were sent here for? I pay rent myself and do not believe it right to do so."

Several others expressed the same sentiment and said they had been warned out to fight and they thought they had to do it. They thanked mother for explaining to them the true conditions of the affair. The Brimstone church at that time was full of men they had made prisoners. They captured every man they could find who would not say "up with the rent." My father was a prisoner in the old church and was taken later to Schoharie where he was kept a prisoner for a week. They captured, also, my brother John and made him a prisoner in the church. Upon mother learning of this she started for the church with some bread and pie. The scene at the church brought tears to her eyes and it also roiled her Dutch blood. "John," she demanded, "you come home with me." A man by the name of Jake Allen spoke up and said: "No, he can't go home with you. Do you think we are going to be effected by the tears of women and children?" Mother then said, "You cannot hold that young boy here; you have no right to do so." Taking her boy by the hand saying "John, you come home with me," she bade her dear husband good by and returned to her home. Many of the posse were not in sympathy with the cause and would not try to capture a man even though they said, "Down with the rent," for they were in sympathy with them. The war did not last long after this but made a great amount of trouble and expense for the community. The Brimstone church was a perfect wreck inside when the trouble ceased. To repair it at this time was a heavy burden on the people. Most of the farmers bought the claims of the land-holders after the disturbance was over.

Isaac Peaslee of Georgetown, California, says:

Smith Peaslee used to go with his basket to feed Scudder when he was hiding on Blenheim Hill. He would go down through that little piece of timber south-east of the old Wickham spring. That route may have been for a guise on the way to the wigwam, which was three hundred yards north-west from the spring. The two pieces of timber were not far apart and the space between grown up to brush. The Delhi posse, when on the Hill, were stationed around the house of Thomas Peaslee, then occupied by John J. Warner. An anti-renter came up the back way, the posse saw him and gave chase. He ran for the fence east of the house, a high stone wall five feet wide. The man scaled it but a member of the posse on horseback, coming to the wall at full speed, was thrown over the fence, landing several feet down the embankment. His party carried him up to the house and it was thought his neck was broken. He was put into a wagon and taken to Delhi. I do not remember whether he lived or not. There were thirty prisoners taken to Gilboa. Taking all in all, the anti-rent war was a good thing for Blenheim Hill and the country interested. It brought the landlords to a settlement and men who went through the conflict were the first to respond to the call for troops in '61. If the anti-rent war had happened after the Civil War it would have been a war of blood. The gang of hoodlums that accompanied the militia would have been wiped off the face of the earth at the first blast of the old tin horn.

Charles Fredenburg of Worcester in memory goes back to boyhood days and says:

My father was Hiram Fredenburg and we lived on Blenheim Ridge during the anti-rent struggle. Father was agent for Russell Forsyth, owner of the Van Rensselaer patent. One day I saw from six to ten horsemen pass my father's house, and I followed them. They stopped at

Amos Loper's shoe shop and dismounted, and I was present when they arrested Loper. Can remember that two of the men were Ezra Syples and Jacob M. Allen. They surprised Loper by sending a farmer to see if he was at home and the messenger was to wave a handkerchief if he was there which the mounted men could see from their position opposite Colby Reed's store. They made the arrest. In regard to Scudder being conducted to Blenheim Hill, it was done Sunday evening after church services. I remember a man came in haste to my father's house and said: "Scudder is coming through! Get an officer and arrest him!" In the afternoon Thomas Vroman went to Moresville with his sorrel horses, riding one and leading the other. In less than an hour after the man came to our house Thomas Vroman rode by on his return in company with a man which proved to be Scudder. I saw them myself. McEntyre, I am quite sure, was not an Indian chief. Amos Loper had a family of boys and there were six boys in my father's family. Loper's boys were "anti-renters" and we called our side "the law and order party." We had many disputes and often would come together and a bloody nose was a frequent result. Our side would make rhymes and we would sing them, and then we would have to run or fight. We didn't run.

John R. Sage of Des Moines, Iowa, writes:

I was too young during that period to take an active part, though old enough to yell like an Indian for the good cause, and I tramped many miles to attend liberty-pole raisings and see the great parades of whole regiments of young and old men dressed in calico and disguised with leather faces. It was a period of tremendous excitement, and the marvel is that there was no armed conflict and bloodshed on the Hill. I was about seven when the anti-renters organized in the old church. My father and older brothers were there, and I remember some of the talk in our family about the big meeting. I recall of my father telling of Benjamin Curtis' remark that he must pray over the matter before taking a part in the conflict. Among the most effective speakers at the pole raising and big meetings were Thomas Peaslee, John Mayham and Amos Loper (my uncle by marriage), who resided in the village of South Blenheim, now South Gilboa. At one of the 4th of July celebrations at Summit, I heard a thrilling anti-rent speech by Hon. Ira Harris of Albany, afterwards U.S. Senator. I recall the fact that by agreement among the anti-rent farmers the dinner horns were not to be used during the "war," except as a signal of the approach of some officer, or posse, to make arrests or serve writs of ejectment. The up-renters, or opponents of the tenants, refused to comply and used their dinner horns in the old way at meal time. This caused the "Indian" boys some amusement for a time. They dressed up and responded to the dinner calls in a manner that was not altogether according to the usage of polite society, clearing of the tables "sans-ceremony." All's well that ends well. The outcome of that conflict was good, and in that case the end justified the means.

CHAPTER XXV

The Manor House

With the purchase of the soil, the tenants on the Blenheim patent and on others of the patroon estates became the absolute owners of the land. Judge Mayham says: "John A. King magnanimously offered to sell his lease-hold interests to the tenants for the sum at which his rent was capitalized and his offer was followed by other landlords. This proposition was accepted by most of the tenants who thus became the owners of the fee of their farms." These purchases were made at different times and on various conditions but in general the price paid was very low.

The men who came into possession of these farms during the decade following the Mexican war forged ahead wonderfully and in a few years became independent, as that term is understood and applied in rural communities. That the anti-rent war contributed directly to this result, there can be no doubt. The people were thoroughly aroused and for several years kept constantly on the alert. This infused energy. When at last they won the battle they set to work with a will and their efforts were rewarded. Thirty years after the close of the conflict, Sheldon Peaslee and Giles S. Champlin were each keeping fifty cows and each worth $20,000. They started as tenants with bare hands. Every acre of Blenheim Hill land came to be occupied by its owner and every farmer prospered.

The John Mayham House
Built during the Anti-Rent War

Any system of land tenure must be judged by its results covering a long period of years. Many Blenheim Hill farms have again
reverted to tenants from year to year or have been abandoned
altogether. The assessed valuation will barely reach $10 per acre.
Evidences of decadence are on every hand. A few homesteads re-
tain their former show of good husbandry but the region as a
whole is desolate. In the light of present conditions it has been
suggested that the old lease-hold system was after all the best.
This must remain a question for the theorist. The social and economic history of the last quarter of a century has not yet been
written; is not, in fact, yet understood. The men who prospered
on Blenheim Hill began in the clearings when the woods came
to the door step and rye grew taller than the blackened stumps.
The fields they made, the homes they established, had no charms
and little value in the eyes of their children's children. The younger

generation went out from a good land to face new conditions. It is doubtful if the old system of a small annual rent, or any system of holding, would re-people the old Backbone.

It must be admitted, however, that there were some good features about the patroon tenures. The best house ever built in Blenheim was erected early in the last century by Judge Lansing, one of the early landlords. It is a grand old mansion today, owned and occupied by Willard Spring, a son of Olney J. Spring. The situation is particularly striking, on a bluff overlooking the Schoharie and fronting the steep and wooded side of Blenheim Hill. Judge Jacob Sutherland resided there and so also did Judge Rosseter, the latter about 1842. When Sheldon Peaslee, Giles S. Champlin, and John R. Sage were boys, a daughter of Judge Sutherland taught a Sunday school at the great manor-house, gathering in the children for miles around. This work was of great and lasting benefit and seems to have been only one of the

The Manor House

many ways in which the resident landlords and their families devoted themselves to the interests of the tenants. It may be that such efforts resulted in a number of the boys becoming lawyers, physicians, and clergymen of distinction.

Life at the old manor-house, in the 40's and earlier, must have been characterized by pomp and luxury. Everything about the old mansion speaks of grandeur,—the great cellars, basement kitchens, and store-rooms; the spacious reception and banquet halls, the grand parlors; the many chambers all provided with open fire-places. Rent day was an education in itself when the tenants were invited to be entertained and to make merry. There surely was a charm about the old life that has altogether disappeared.

The story of the anti-rent war as herein narrated has been written after many interviews with men connected with the events described, a careful examination of original documents, papers, and records, a study of family traditions, and a review of the very limited number of books and sketches heretofore written on the subject. Of the latter source of information it may be said that a few authors have contributed something to the available accounts of the war, but all such are fragmentary essays, hidden away, for the most part, in isolated chapters in forgotten old books. The present narrative, published serially in the *Jefferson Courier and Schoharie County Chronicle* from April 6 to October 11, 1906, is the first and only complete history of the conflict ever written. The story forms an episode in the author's larger history of Blenheim Hill, a work covering the whole period of the life of that community from the settlement of the Blenheim patent to the present time.

In conclusion, a short recapitulation of the salient features of the anti-rent agitation may be briefly stated. In colonial times a large proportion of the farming land of New York came into the ownership of a few great proprietors. On these lands the leasehold system grew up, a product partly of the feudal ideas of the great land-owners, partly of the poverty of the farmers as a class. The lands, when first settled by tenants, were in general entirely unimproved, and the farmers who cleared them felt, with evident justice, that it was they who had created the flourishing country which had taken the place of the early wilderness. The poverty and misfortune of individual tenants, and the growing wealth and independence of the landlords as a class, tended to create dissatisfaction, especially when the proprietors, about 1840, attempted a more rigorous enforcement of their contract rights. United resistance on the part of tenants followed. Anti-rent associations were formed, and finally disorder and lawlessness, strife in the courts, at the polls, and in the legislature ensued. Portions of the state were declared in insurrection and the militia called out. The anti-rent party held the balance of power at the polls for several years and for a time dominated state politics. The demands of the tenants culminated in the changes made in the constitution of 1846. The objects of the movement were essentially just and highly desirable, the men engaged in the agitation were sincere, and the results were advantageous.